The Year of the Poet VIII

February 2021

The Poetry Posse

inner child press, ltd.

The Poetry Posse 2021

Gail Weston Shazor

Shareef Abdur Rasheed

Teresa E. Gallion

hülya n. yılmaz

Kimberly Burnham

Tzemin Ition Tsai

Elizabeth Esguerra Castillo

Jackie Davis Allen

Joe Paire

Caroline 'Ceri' Nazareno

Ashok K. Bhargava

Alicja Maria Kuberska

Swapna Behera

Albert 'Infinite' Carrasco

Eliza Segiet

William S. Peters, Sr.

~ * ~

In order to maintain each poet's authentic voice, this volume has not undergone the scrutiny of editing. Please take time to indulge each contributor for their own creativity and aspirations to convey their uniqueness.

hülya n. yılmaz, Ph.D.
Director of Editing ~
Inner Child Press International

General Information

The Year of the Poet VIII
February 2021 Edition

The Poetry Posse

1st Edition : 2021

Publisher Information
1st Edition : Inner Child Press
intouch@innerchildpress.com
www.innerchildpress.com

ISBN-13 : 978-1-952081-41-5 (inner child press, ltd.)

$ 12.99

WHAT WOULD LIFE BE WITHOUT A LITTLE POETRY?

Dedication

This Book is dedicated to

Humanity, Peace & Poetry

the Power of the Pen

can effectuate change!

&

The Poetry Posse

past, present & future

our Patrons and Readers

the Spirit of our Everlasting Muse

In the darkness of my life
I heard the music
I danced . . .
and the Light appeared
and I dance

Janet P. Caldwell

Table of Contents

Foreword   ix

Preface   xiii

The Feature   xv

The Poetry Posse

Gail Weston Shazor   1

Alicja Maria Kuberska   7

Jackie Davis Allen   13

Tezmin Ition Tsai   19

Shareef Abdur – Rasheed   25

Kimberly Burnham   33

Elizabeth Esguerra Castillo   39

Joe Paire   45

hülya n. yılmaz   51

Teresa E. Gallion   61

Table of Contents . . . *continued*

Ashok K. Bhargava   67

Caroline Nazareno-Gabis   73

Swapna Behera   79

Albert Carassco   85

Eliza Segiet   91

William S. Peters, Sr.   97

February's Featured Poets   109

T.Ramesh Babu   111

Ruchida Barman   117

Neptune Barman   123

Faleeha Hassan   131

Inner Child News   139

Other Anthological Works   167

Foreword

February is **Black History Month**. It is an annual celebration of achievements by African Americans and a time for recognizing the central role of blacks in U.S. history. The event grew out of "Negro History Week," the brainchild of a noted historian Carter G. Woodson. Also known as the African American History Month, it has received official recognition from governments in the United States and Canada, and more recently has been observed in Ireland, the Netherlands, and the United Kingdom by remembering important people and events in the history of the African diaspora.

For the month of February, Inner Child poets are invited to celebrate Black History month by pondering upon the recreation of a mural of Emory Douglas and Richard Bell's *"We Can Be Heroes"* in 2014. It depicts a particular moment during the 1968 Mexico Olympic Games when Australian sprinter, Peter Norman stood in solidarity with African American sportsmen Tommie Smith and John Carlos to protest discrimination and inequality. This beautiful mural is located in Brisbane, Australia. Their collaborative project focuses on the Black Power movement of America and the Indigenous rights movements of Australia.

Poetry like contemporary art s to reimagine and embrace new creative forms of activism that responds to social justice issues. 'Artists have a way of instantly communicating essence, almost like a language' says Emory Douglas who was an artist with the Black Panther Party for nearly 20 years starting in 1967. The controversial Richard Bell is one of Australia's most renowned Indigenous artists. With a penchant for sarcasm he explores stereotypes and racism through his self-titled 'Liberation art'. Douglas may be considered in a similar vein as the Minister of Culture in the Black Panther Party who was also the art director, designer and main illustrator for the Black Panther newspaper, creating iconic images that represented the struggles in America during the 1960s and 1970s.

The 2020 has been a very difficult year. The challenges of surviving the pandemic made us aware of the potent interplay of self-isolation, social distancing, systemic oppression and marginalization. It heralded the awakening of a world ready to respond to the social justice issues that had been overlooked for a long time. We realized that truth is not what we want it to be; it is what it is. We need to liberate ourselves by unlearning oppressive social systems, and restoring and repairing our social contract with one another.

A clenched fist embodies determination to achieve social Justice with fresh perspectives. In his autobiography, *'Silent Gesture'*, Tommie Smith writes that the clenched fist is not just a gesture of "Black Power" but also a "human rights" salute because oppression spares no body: oppressor or the oppressed. The questions to ponder for us are: How do we become the change we wish to see and how can we stay grounded and centered and increase our capacity for sustainable change? The aim of literature and art is to represent not the outward appearance of things but their inward significance.

Ashok K. Bhargava

President, Writers International Network Canada

bhargava2000@yahoo.com

World Healing World Peace
2020

Poets for Humanity

Now Available

www.innerchildpress.com/world-healing-world-peace-poetry

www.worldhealingworldpeacepoetry.com

www.worldhealingworldpeacefoundation.org

Preface

Dear Family and Friends,

So, here we are, beginning our eighth year of monthly publication of *The Year of the Poet*. Amazing how much effort has been given by all the poets, to include the various members of *The Poetry Posse* and all the wonderful featured poets from all over our world. For myself, it has been and continues to be a great honor to be a part of this wonderful cooperative effort.

Last year, 2020 has been challenging for many of us throughout the year. We at *Inner Child Press International* were busy. We envisioned our role where the arts meet humanity to continue doing what we were good at . . . publishing. We managed to not only produce and publish this series, *The Year of the Poet* each month, but we were also very proactive in the arena of human and social consciousness. We were able to produce several other anthologies to include: World Healing, World Peace 2020; CORONA . . . social distancing; The Heart of a Poet; W.A.R. . . we are revolution; Poetry, the Best of 2020. Going forward, we are seeking to invest in the same or greater effort towards contributing to a 'conscious humanity'. We, poets and writers do have something to say about it all, and we intend to do so in any and every way we can. So stay tuned . . .

Bill

William S. Peters, Sr.

Publisher
Inner Child Press International

www.innerchildpress.com

PS

Do Not forget about the World Healing, World
Peace Poetry initiative for 2022. Mark your
calendars. Submissions will be opening . . .
September 1st 2021

Past volumes are vailable here

www.worldhealingworldpeacepoetry.com

**For Free Downloads of Previous Issues of
The Year of the Poet**

www.innerchildpress.com/the-year-of-the-poet

Emory Douglas Art

February 2021

For Black History Month in the United States, we feature ekphrastic poems focused on the work of Emory Douglas, who was born May 24, 1943. An American artist, Douglas worked with the Black Panther Party for nearly 20 years starting in 1967. An art director, designer, and illustrator, Douglas created images that became symbolic of an earlier era's Black Lives Matter.

https://en.wikipedia.org/wiki/Emory_Douglas

"Artists have a way of instantly communicating essence. Things are made clear, almost like a language, and so art is a powerful tool to communicate with the community." ~Emory Douglas

Emory Douglas mural painted in Nottingham as part of Jean Genet exhibition at Nottingham Contemporary. Summer 2011

https://commons.wikimedia.org/wiki/File:Genet-mural-2011.jpg

Poets . . .
sowing seeds in the
Conscious Garden of Life,
that those who have yet to come
may enjoy the Flowers.

Poets, Writers . . . know that we are the enchanting magicians that nourishes the seeds of dreams and thoughts . . . it is our words that entice the hearts and minds of others to believe there is something grand about the possibilities that life has to offer and our words tease it forth into action . . . for you are the Poet, the Writer to whom the Gift of Words has been entrusted . . .

~ wsp

poetry is . . .

Poetry succeeds where instruction fails.

~ wsp

I Fly

because I Can

...said the Dreamer to the world.

Gail Weston Shazor

This is a creative promise ~ my pen will speak to and for the world. Enamored with letters and respectful of their power, I have been writing for most of my life. A mother, daughter, sister and grandmother I give what I have been given, greatfilledly.

Author of . . .

"An Overstanding of an Imperfect Love"
&
Notes from the Blue Roof

Lies My Grandfathers Told Me

available at Inner Child Press.

www.facebook.com/gailwestonshazor
www.innerchildpress.com/gail-weston-shazor
navypoet1@gmail.com

Power

Electricities crackle in the firmament
Motions of creation
Shed a blue light across the horizon
And in the ebbing of this day
Clay moves
So I stand mystified

Covering my eyes against
The sharp glare
I wait the brush strokes
To reveal majesty ordained
Luminosity
Of firmed dirt

Baked under a sun
Powered by the cloak
Of darkness
I witnessed the birth
Of my mate
Of the black man

Day 3

Yada defines my roof perch today
 And all the adjacent stonework
 None of it covered and I can see
 The buildings bones, the beginnings
 Irregularly settled into the form of the day

Saturdays are quiet in unfolding
I know Mother has long been at market
Arranging teas, tisanes and brown jars
Her first fruits for early risers
And I realize I am late for her gifts
Mother's seconds seem so much earlier
Than mine are on such breaking mornings
And maybe on the beginning of all days

You accept my easing into this place
Placing it above you and I-first
Hermeneutically sealing my needs
For I spoke this to you on the first rising

This need to be whole and in place
 That morning, with the sea close enough to kiss
 Long before ascending ninety-nine
 Yada-In the beginning-first knowledge

anticipation...sedoka

I have been waiting

On a 'round the way black man

To come and take the edge off

No need to share names

For I will never be yours

My heart has been lost at sea

Alicja
Maria
Kuberska

.

Alicja Maria Kuberska – awarded Polish poetess, novelist, journalist, editor.

She is a member of the Polish Writers Associations in Warsaw, Poland and IWA Bogdani, Albania. She is also a member of directors' board of Soflay Literature Foundation, Our Poetry Archive (India) and Cultural Ambassador for Poland (Inner Child Press, USA)

Her poems have been published in numerous anthologies and magazines in : Poland, Czech Republic, Slovakia, Hungary,Ukraina, Belgium, Bulgaria, Albania, Spain, the UK, Italy, the USA, Canada, the UK, Argentina, Chile, Peru, Israel, Turkey, India, Uzbekistan, South Korea, Taiwan, China, Australia, South Africa, Zambia, Nigeria

She received two medals - the Nosside UNESCO Competition in Italy (2015) and European Academy of Science Arts and Letters in France (2017). Ahe also received a reward of international literary competition in Italy „ Tra le parole e 'elfinito" (2018). She was announced a poet of the 2017 year by Soflay Literature Foundation (2018).She also received : Bolesław Prus Prize Poland (2019), Culture Animator Poland (2019) and first prize Premio Internazionale di Poesia Poseidonia- Paestrum Italy (2019).

The Black

Anger and soreness are black
and rebellion has black color too.
Unspeakable words
shout loudly.
They make you frown,
clench your fists
and put your hand up.

Injustice hurts.
Faces freeze in grimace
of apparent calm.
People similar
to the black panthers
are waiting to jump
to cry out their pain.

Tea Time

Peace and color emerge from the tea bag.
Silver leaves unfold in the boiling water,
There is a scent of jasmine flowers
And sweet fruity notes ring out.

It doesn't take much to invite home
The memory of the Eden and the sun.
While we are sipping some tea we tell stories .
 Our time slows down and takes on an aroma.

Hidden Gateway

I drink from the cup of your longing.
The energy of thoughts gives flavor.
I absorb the sadness, bitterness,
And sense a little bit of hope
That it may not always be the case.

Once the cup is empty
- Pour another type of wine!
Meet the sweetness of grapes
And sun-ripened expectations.

Life has got not only a bitter taste
And is not made of duty's signposts.
Somewhere in the wall of hopelessness
There is a hidden gateway to the Garden of Eden.
Remember, it is never closed

Jackie

Davis

Allen

Jackie Davis Allen, otherwise known as Jacqueline D. Allen or Jackie Allen, grew up in the Cumberland Mountains of Appalachia. As the next eldest daughter of a coal miner father and a stay at home mother, she was the first in her family to attend and graduate from college. Her siblings, in their own right, are accomplished, though she is the only one, to date, that has discovered the gift of writing.

Graduating from Radford University, with a Bachelors of Science degree in Early Education, she taught in both public and private schools. For over a decade she taught private art classes to children both in her home and at a local Art and Framing Shop where she also sold her original soft sculptured Victorian dolls and original christening gowns.

She resides in northern Virginia with her husband, taking much needed get-aways to their mountain home near the Blue Ridge Mountains, a place that evokes memories of days spent growing up in the Appalachian Mountains.

A lover of hats, she has worn many. Following marriage to her college sweetheart, and as wife, mother, grandmother, teacher, tutor, artist, writer, poet and crafter, she is a lover of art and antiques, surrounding herself, always, with books, seeking to learn more.

In 2015 she authored *Looking for Rainbows, Poetry, Prose and Art*, and in 2017, *Dark Side of the Moon*. Both books of mostly narrative poetry were published by Inner Child Press and were edited by hulya n. yilmaz.

in 2019, No Illusions.Through the Looking Glass, which was nominated to be considered for a Pulitzer Prize by the publisher and editor of InnerChild Press, ltd.

http://www.innerchildpress.com/jackie-davis-allen.php
jackiedavisallen.com

Definition's Manifestation

Emory Douglas, famous
As an artist, painted
A picture on a wall

Three men standing, proud
Powerful athletes, each
A winner: first, second, third

With raised hands high, aware
In celebratory manner, understanding
Demonstrating the definition

Of how these men together, created
An image that depicts more,
Describes more than could a thousand words

Motivated, Determined

I have known hunger...
The searching need
A reminder of some emptiness~

> Yet I will not be defeated
> Nor bow down to its claim.

O yes, I have known hunger.
With voice most vociferous
It identifies me as determined.

> It pulls me up by its great need
> And calls me by my name.

I have known hunger
And its penetrating ache...
A reminder of a gnawing inside.

> Yet my eyes focus on the prize
> And I ignore thoughts of blame.

O yes, I have known hunger.
The immensity tattoos itself~
Identifies me as motivated.

> It whispers in my ear that
> In effort there is no shame.

I have known hunger
And its unrelenting pain~
More than pages of speculation

> That would spell defeat,
> That might be insult to fame.

O, yes. I have known hunger.
The deprivation manifests itself,
Identifies me as most determined.

> It reminds me to honor my gift, and
> That hunger can lead to acclaim.

Sleeping Sheep

In a world where heads
Are calling for reprograming
As a solution, I ask, why? For what purpose?
For whom? On whose authority?
May the Almighty deliver us from evil.

There are many who are fearful,
Concerned that to speak up
Would single them out.
As free thinking individuals?
What happened to freedom of expression?

Standing on bedrock of principle,
Rejecting violence of activists,
Some choose not the world
Of fiction, where "equality"
Means "ideology of sameness".

Of those preferring to think
For themselves, they resist the media's
Cadre of propagandists.
And the ensuing, inevitable
Loss of common sense.

Of the fictional, imagine an intentional novel
Yet to be fulfilled, penned metaphorically:
Consider the inking possibility of 1984's stamp
On all foreheads. Might not that wake up
The snoring band of sleeping sheep?

Tzemin
Ition
Tsai

Dr. Tzemin Ition Tsai (蔡澤民博士) was born in Republic of China, in 1957. He holds a Ph.D. in Chemical Engineering and two Masters of Science in Applied Mathematics and Chemical Engineering. He is a professor at Asia University (Taiwan), editor of "Reading, Writing and Teaching" academic text. He also writes the long-term columns for Chinese Language Monthly in Taiwan.

He is a scholar with a wide range of expertise, while maintaining a common and positive interest in science, engineering and literature member. He is also an editor of "Reading, Writing and Teaching" academic text and a columnist for *Chinese Language Monthly'* in Taiwan

He has won many national literary awards. His literary works have been anthologized and published in books, journals, and newspapers in more than 40 countries and have been translated into more than a dozen languages.

Black Strips

Under the gaze of two eyes
It's been a while
I remembered after all
That must be draw in a way
An understandable way to attract the widest audience
Without losing the substance or insight of what is
　　represented

Image inspiration
Very graphically enhanced
A revolution in the black resistance
The art of activists keeps pace with the times
Not to strengthen the cultural dead end of postmodern
　　nostalgia
His inspiration is only to increase the possibility of new
　　revolutionary culture

It's like an existential hope
Induce the truth in depravation
This black outline of trying
Nothing more than
Want to construct a visual mythology of power
For people who felt powerless and victimized
Notorious for voyeuristic and patronizing
Can be seen as respect and affection
Can be outlined in the warnings of the world
Black lines dyed by other colors are never allowed

What Spring Told Me

Once the engagement ring went through my ring finger
Spring was keen on going back on his word
Jumping, like the wine on the lake
What a thing originally only cared about being idle and
    melancholy
Finally, must calculated
How much happy soul I have left

That night
Deep into the dark tent
Spring smiled hard at me
Carefully only one step away from the kingdom full of
    spring water
That once glorious midnight
Began to become silent and dim

A happy Chinese New Year, whizzing through the window
    above my head
Waking up, feels like even in sleeping
Spring was not let go
Surprised by the lonely dormant period
Was passion intertwined in summer immersed in departing
    spring?
I sat down and waited and walked along the river where I
    wanted to reach

As walked in, Winding road
Covered in the shade of trees, marveled
Downstream ditch swallows the torture of dreams until
Woke up
The storm reminds me of swallows and the loneliness in the
    middle of the night
A lonely person who sheds tears alone
Yes, lonely
My soul became no longer happy that day

The Stone Bridge

Beside the stream, I saw the beating stream
brought me back to my childhood at a pace that is too real
The memory that still continues
The trapeze in dreams never landed
The god of wind seems to always forget to stop
Reminded me of the hyacinth message flying on the water
The petals thrown on the hydrofoil
Multiple rhythms
Dancing beyond water vapor
Sputtered gently on the skirts of visitors on the bridge
The sharp beak of a flamingo that never cruises
Pecking down the lowest note in the stars of last night
Was pleased to jump for joy
What else can be more purely hidden in
Inboard, a footprint
I found the paw
I heard sliding sound
Buzzing
The reflection in the water looked so tiny
Reminded me, don't forget to long for the reality of the
high surface of this stone bridge

Shareef Abdur Rasheed

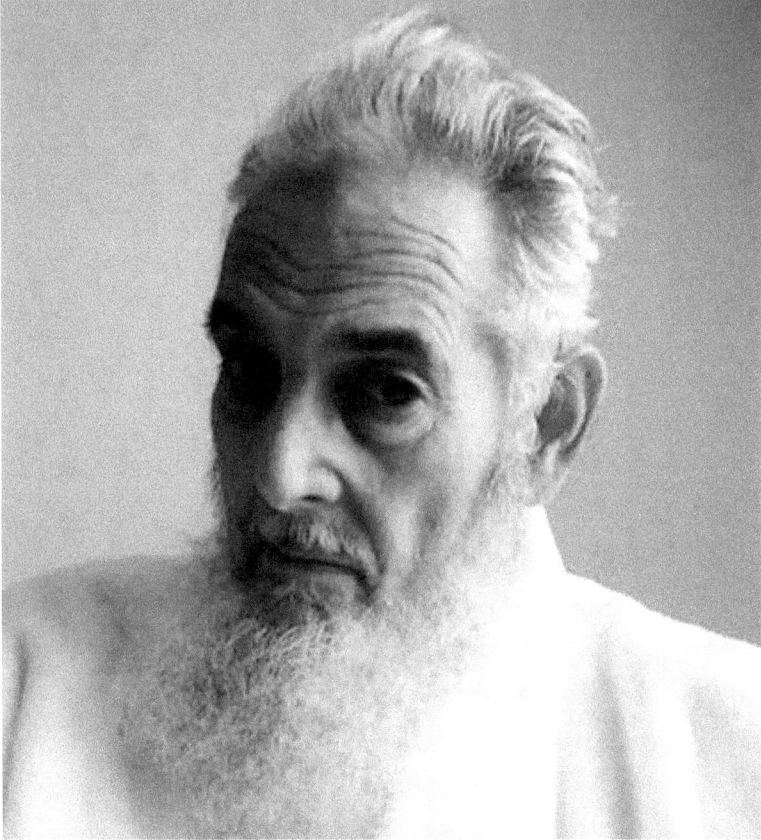

Shareef Abdur-Rasheed, AKA Zakir Flo was born and raised in Brooklyn, New York. His education includes Brooklyn College, Suffolk County Community College and Makkah, Saudi Arabia. He is a Veteran of the Viet Nam era, where in 1969 he reverted to his now reverently embraced Islamic Faith. He is very active in the Islamic community and beyond with his teachings, activism and his humanity.

Shareef's spiritual expression comes through the persona of "Zakir Flo" . Zakir is Arabic for "To remind". Never silent, Shareef Abdur-Rasheed is always dropping science, love, consciousness and signs of the time in rhyme.

Shareef is the Patriarch of the Abdur-Rasheed Family with 9 Children (6 Sons and 3 Daughters) and 41 Grandchildren (24 Boys and 17 Girls).

For more information about Shareef, visit his personal FaceBook Page at :

https://www.facebook.com/shareef.abdurrasheed1
https://zakirflo.wordpress.com

Emory Douglas

gifted graphic artist,
revolutionary
artist using unique
imagery exposing
evil measures that
devils impose
for wealth, power,
pleasure
that being oppression,
degrees of slavery
visual stimulation
subject: targeted nation
brought light to struggle
through artful expression
expose agenda hidden
in dark corners
shed light on plight
oppressed peoples
Africans in AmeriKKKa
through power of art
truth rendered
and ooh ya i remember
talking powerful piece
" We Can Be Heroes "
collaboration with
Australian indigenous
artist Richard Bell
depiction: Australian Peter
Norman standing in solidarity
with American Black Athletes
John Carlos, Tommie Smith
on the medal stand
not just for winning medals
notwithstanding Olympic
medals at that in track

at 1968 Olympic Games
Mexico City
That wasn't their objective
glory of victory
applause, adulation
not at all, instead
attention to the cause
liberation of oppressed nation
i remember like it was yesterday
more than 52 years of yesterdays
They, Carlos and Smith raised
their black gloved fist on medal
stand,
yes, indeed Black Power salute
and oh yes, they got the boot
banned from Olympic Village
for telling truth to power
in middle of medal hour

food4thought = education

Afterwards

so, they come back to the snakes
under attack John Carlos,
Tommie Smith Olympic medalist
human rights activists
two of the world's best at what
they do
decided to stand up for truth, justice
instead of getting all that's coming
to us
Douglas reproduced the essence
of that moment in time that brought
attention to severe oppression
sustained for many generations
by African peoples treated less then
human denied equality
by so called white folk who claimed
they believed what Christ thought
you will be judged individually,
collectively as a society
how you treated the least of thee
in terms of status socially,
economically, politically
hypocrisy exposed
in what Emory Douglas art proposed
both Carlos and Smith were
condemned as pariah's
not like being born black males
in United Snakes wasn't enough
then stakes became much more tough
the difference between hypocrisy
and service to all humanity.

food4thought = education

time..,

squared is where?
mankind revels
mankind rebels
mankind has fell
mankind flirts with hell
time squared is where?
has it brought us far or near?
how fast went the years
count those no longer
here
the signs beware
the signs beware
the signs are everywhere
count those no longer here
be mindful of " God Fear "
the time has rendered
mankind unaware
life neither here nor there
that's not why your here
be mindful of "God Fear"
time allotted unknown
but what sense of urgency
shown?
way we live you'd think it's
something we own
no man will escape results of
seeds sown
did it amount to life blown?
this is how we go home?
the glitter has no substance
like foam
like the water you saw in
the desert was sand blown
an illusion like the things
you think you own

take heed
the only thing you need
in your grave alone
Righteous Deeds and
mercy
food4thought = education

food4thought = education

Kimberly Burnham

A brain health expert with a PhD in Integrative Medicine, Kimberly Burnham has lived in tropical Colombia; in Belgium during the Vietnam War; in Japan teaching businessmen English; in diverse international Toronto, Canada; and several places in the US. Now, she's in Spokane, WA with her wife, Elizabeth, two sets of twins (age 11 & 14) and three dogs. Her recent book, *Awakenings: Peace Dictionary, Language and the Mind, a Daily Brain Health Program* includes the word for peace in hundreds of languages. Her poetry weaves through 80+ volumes of *The Year of the Poet, Inspired by Gandhi, Women Building the World*, and *A Woman's Place in the Dictionary*. She is currently working on several ekphrastic writing projects. One is a novel, *Art Thief Cracks Healing Code for Parkinson's Disease* and the other is non-fiction, *Using Ekphrastic Fiction Writing and Poetry to Create Interest and Promote Artists, Writers, and Poets*.

http://www.NerveWhisperer.Solutions

https://healthy-brain.medium.com/bears-at-the-window-of-climate-change-d1fb403eeaf3

Fists Raised

In anger fists raised
batter the world

In solidarity fists
reassure those by my side

Raised in a gesture
of Olympic proportion triumph

Fists show power and pride
in accomplishments

But the world sees only the gesture
movement and expression

Assumes the feelings yet
only I know my own intentions

Black Panther Haiku

Red bricks white canvas

two yellow suns shine on black

men trying to move

Right and Left Brain Together

We dance from the left
with logic and linear thinking
focusing on facts and numbers
words and sights driving
the sequence of how we act

We leap from the right
full of imagination and creativity
following intuition
it just felt right
dream about how it will feel
emotions hard to put into words

Different sides
struggling for dominance
fighting for time to think and feel
linear facts or intuitive imagination
each will take us far
the farthest
the best
work together

Elizabeth E. Castillo

Elizabeth Esguerra Castillo is a multi-awarded and an Internationally-Published Contemporary Author/Poet and a Professional Writer / Creative Writer / Feature Writer / Journalist / Travel Writer from the Philippines. She has 2 published books, "Seasons of Emotions" (UK) and "Inner Reflections of the Muse", (USA). Elizabeth is also a co-author to more than 60 international anthologies in the USA, Canada, UK, Romania, India. She is a Contributing Editor of Inner Child Magazine, USA and an Advisory Board Member of Reflection Magazine, an international literary magazine. She is a member of the American Authors Association (AAA) and PEN International.

Web links:

Facebook Fan Page

https://free.facebook.com/ElizabethEsguerraCastillo

Google Plus

https://plus.google.com/u/0/+ElizabethCastillo

My Color is Black

My skin is black
And I matter,
Allow me to enjoy my rights
Don't let me succumb to fright.

My color is universal,
I am proud of my race
We all have a place in this world,
Coming from one Source.

When I Can No Longer Breathe You

silence permeates the air.
a chilly-like atmosphere envelopes this dark night
with the stars and the valiant moon's light,
the ones only illuminating
this maze-like path to nowhere...
you were once a strong presence in my life
made sense to a once weary soul
wrap up in the darkness, alone, and bewildered
an echo whispering sweet nothings to my ears.

when I can no longer breathe you,
'tis the time the heart chooses not to feel anymore.
when I can no longer feel the closeness of you
'tis the time the heart chooses to just sleep and wait for
eternity.

when there's no more beautiful coincidences
binding our hearts and souls together,
I will just choose to be in oblivion
be a roaming restless spirit
waiting for the day we'll be reunited in heaven.

time may heal a bereaved heart
but to love again is a question
when I choose not to feel.

When I can no longer breathe you
I'll ask the angels to send my love
And sing the music I made for you
For you to know that my love
Goes beyond the grave,
A love that will continue in the next lifetime.

Journey to the Future

Brave men reaching for the stars,
A journey beyond imagination
Taking flight to a distant place
Making a mark to change the world.

A once unthinkable voyage,
Now within man's reach
A journey to the future
An indisputable feat of human kind.

Let's celebrate this journey to the future,
And let it be known by generations to come
We can reach the stars,
And dare take flight.

Joe
Paire

Joseph L Paire' aka Joe DaVerbal Minddancer . . .
is a quiet man, born in a time where civil liberties
were a walk on thin ice. He's been a victim of his
own shyness often sidelined in his own quest for
love. He became the observer, charting life's path.
Taking note of the why, people do what they do. His
writings oft times strike a cord with the
dormant strings of the reader. His pen the rosined
bow drawn across the mind. He comes full-frontal
or in the subtlest way, always expressing in a way
that stimulate the senses.

www.facebook.com/joe.minddancer

There's an "H" in Humanity

Silent gestures speak words to the hearing impaired.
Body languages speak of want and need.
We see what we believe.
We heed to what we hear.
Experience guides the mind's eye.

Prejudiced eyes like blinders for a racehorse,
Cause a little bit of discourse.
Of course, I've seen it happen when it happened.
But my caption as it were back then.
I was captured by the heart back when.

With an SUV parked just below this scene.
Black history or black misery, the thoughts just flood in.
I got a sense of pride when my eyes saw the movement.
I found this image to be intuitive.
A small taste of freedom only to be ruled again.

Some just see hooligans but that's the fool in them.
When I look at this image now,
I see I've been schooled again.
Right fist raised, left fist raised,
two strong arms formed an "H" there's an H in humanity.

The Terror Within

My capital is under siege from people who look like me.
I never thought I'd live to see the days of Paul Revere.
The British weren't coming, but their intent was clear.
There was no need for a midnight ride.
They weren't throwing tea in offence of taxations.
They were throwing their own people out.
Based on lies from the leaders of their palpitations
Years of calculations, years of misinformation

The years of segregation you were okay with that.
Michigan was just a test to fill you in the belly of
the Trojan horse, Moscow Mitch had a new voice.
It's funny, but it's not.
When you shared the thoughts and plots
Rule of law? I think not, Isis was taught by their leader.
Off with their heads, Jim Crow laws for us instead
Held-up to the hilt on Capitol Hill.

But when it's your blood being spilled
The enemy within is revealed.
Choked out necks, for selling cigarettes.
So, justice has been peaking at the rest of us.
The perceived majority have become the despots.
There was so much turmoil over a stained blue dress.
But the killing of democracy let me take a guess.
The power of the vote proved to be actual power.

To destroy within, in hopes to save those ivory towers.
When the twin towers fell, we immediately went sour.
Now you're supporting the very thing we feared.
It's clear the terror within.

Reflections

I need to get to myself but that's the problem.
I've become pure thought.
Years of observing one tends to blend.
In the walls of our own making
Hearts breaking over the antics of a TV. Show

Soap opera's and drama's
Comedies' come in the form of life's mishaps.
Perhaps if I were more than I
That would be a lie.

Mirror, mirror on the wall
Will you shut up once and for all?
I neglect you because you speak truth.
You see through me like I see through wires.

I can't deflect of you no matter how I've tried.
Peacock power never lasts.
Those devoted to the same never fast.
But I'm the one who's gotta ask my reflection.

hülya

n.

yılmaz

Professor Emerita (Humanities, Penn State, USA), hülya n. yılmaz [sic] is a published tri-lingual author, literary translator, and Director of Editing Services (Inner Child Press International, USA). Her work has appeared in numerous anthologies of global endeavors and was presented at poetry events in the U.S. and abroad. In 2018, the WIN of British Colombia, Canada honored yılmaz with a literary excellence award. Her two poems remain permanently installed in *Telepoem Booth* (USA). hülya finds it vital for everyone to understand a deeper sense of self, and writes creatively to attain a comprehensive awareness for and development of our humanity.

Writing Web Site
https://hulyanyilmaz.com/

Editing Web Site
https://hulyasfreelancing.com

A Simple and Silent Gesture

It is August 26 in the year of 2016
in the good ole US of A.
Colin Rand Kaepernick sits in the bench
during the anthem in San Francisco
to raise awareness . . .
because "the country oppresses black people
and people of color."
He was known not to have stood for the anthem before.

That date passes by.

Writers of headlines get busy,
when Kaepernick sits down again a day later.

Reactions are two-fold: some condemn him,
and others applaud.

The NFL speaks up,
citing the lack of any requirement on their behalf
for their athletes to stand up for the anthem.

After three days, former NFL player
and ex-Green Beret Nate Boyer has a suggestion
for this young man of higher consciousness:
"kneel rather than sit."

Kaepernick kneels before a game on September 1st, 2016
and goes on record with his plan for a donation
of $1 million to organizations that support his intent,
as I have noted earlier, "to raise awareness"
for the centuries-long systemic racism in the country.

September 11, 2016 marks the first full day
of the regular season.
Several players kneel during the anthem.

On Sept. 27, 2016, Kaepernick becomes the subject
of harsh criticism from the Republican presidential
candidate Donald Trump.
The young man responds: "He always says make America
great again. Well, America has never been great for people
of color. That's something that needs to be addressed. Let's
make America great for the first time."

Kaepernick plays his final NFL game on January 1st, 2017.
The 49ers plan to cut him.
He opts out of his contract instead.

The month of September of the same year
witnesses players' kneeling before
and / or during the anthem
without the civil rights activist in the league.

In the following month,
Kaepernick files a grievance against NFL team owners.
He cites collusion to keep him out of the league.

The powers that be, unfortunately, have a final say.
NFL season ends on December 31, 2017,
having made certain that this epic role model
for equal justice remains unemployed.
Less than a year afterward, NFL owners construct a rule
banning kneeling during the anthem.
It is 'president' Trump now . . . as he has made it
into the People's House. He applauds the divisive initiative.
NFL owners soon retract the rushed rule
because of its divisiveness.

As the second straight season begins –
sans the name "Kaepernick" on a roster,
some players still kneel . . .

The third NFL season enters the world's calendar,
and ends eventually.
No Kaepernick.

Following the murder of George Floyd, a black man,
on May 25, 2020, nationwide protests begin.
Numerous other sports organizations
join the cause of awareness,
to include the NBA, Baseball, and many more.
Kaepernick offers support.

A few months later, the NFL apologizes, denounces racism
and delivers a promise to further promote social justice.

Thank you for your simple and silent gesture,
dear Mr. Kaepernick.
Your gentle voice was and continues to be
loud enough to stay at the core
of many an equality-for all-seeking soul.
Hopefully, for us all, generations to come
will embrace your contribution to humanity,
understanding and knowing that social injustice
is our common enemy.
Thank you for showing this 'white' woman
that which we all-inclusively must fear.
So, in humble solidarity,
I, too, kneel.
Ever so respectfully.

Emory Douglas

1968
Summer Olympics
The medalists' podium for the 200-meter race

America's own two Black athletes,
Tommie Smith and John Carlos –
One, the recipient of the gold medal;
The other, a silver-medalist

Visual history depicts these winners' fists
Inside black gloves as they raise them into air

To bring to the attention of the world
The centuries-long oppression of Blacks,
AKA the good ole American way

As Smith and Carlos make their unspoken voices heard,
Their medals are being taken away

Standing against the brutally discriminatory
and fear-, hatred- and violence-filled white-domination
is enough reason to strip them both
of their justly earned honors,
you say?

Nay!

A white Australian runner, Peter Norman –
A silver-medalist, chooses to stay with his fellow athletes,
Though sans fist, to show solidarity
He thus lends hope to humanity
And reminds us all of the foundation of our existence:
Unity within diversity. Unconditionally. All-inclusively.

Watching unjust actions unfold for even one of us silently
Is, after all, complicity. Put simply.

Still . . .
The Black athletes
Get their Olympic medals stripped off
They had, however, earned them justly

Promising careers, ruined . . .
In the hands of the white powers that be
How about the rights to practice Civil Rights advocacy?
Huh, what a laugh!
Such freedom for Blacks does not come for free!

In the year of 2014,
A visual art project, "We Can Be Heroes",
Makes waves across the borders of many a country
The piece is crafted collaboratively
Between the Australian artist Richard Bell
And the American graphic designer Emory Douglas

Bell and Douglas not only eternalize
For the 1968 Olympic medalists
Their moments of protest on an Olympic-athlete stage,
The stance they took against discrimination and inequality;
But also demonstrate injustices to be witnessed globally

As it is evident throughout the volume in your possession,
Our collective efforts geared toward poeticizing
Some segments of the once diligently-recorded reality
Jointly, we are anon sharing the marvel of a phenomenon;
Namely, how Bell's concept of 'Liberation Art',
Coupled with Douglas' talent in design and illustration,
Grew larger than life and entered the annals of history
In the form of a silent yet utterly vocal iconography

Enough Is Enough!

Medieval times have passed

Try the now that's here:

The 21st century!

hülya n. yılmaz

Teresa E. Gallion

Teresa E. Gallion was born in Shreveport, Louisiana and moved to Illinois at the age of 15. She completed her undergraduate training at the University of Illinois Chicago and received her master's degree in Psychology from Bowling Green State University in Ohio. She retired from New Mexico state government in 2012.

She moved to New Mexico in 1987. While writing sporadically for many years, in 1998 she started reading her work in the local Albuquerque poetry community. She has been a featured reader at local coffee houses, bookstores, art galleries, museums, libraries, Outpost Performance Space, the Route 66 Festival in 2001 and the State of Oklahoma's Poetry Festival in Cheyenne, Oklahoma in 2004. She occasionally hosts an open mic.

Teresa's work is published in numerous Journals and anthologies. She has two CDs: *On the Wings of the Wind* and *Poems from Chasing Light*. She has published three books: *Walking Sacred Ground, Contemplation in the High Desert* and *Chasing Light.*

Chasing Light was a finalist in the 2013 New Mexico/Arizona Book Awards.

The surreal high desert landscape and her personal spiritual journey influence the writing of this Albuquerque poet. When she is not writing, she is committed to hiking the enchanted landscapes of New Mexico. You may preview her work at

http://bit.ly/1aIVPNq or *http://bit.ly/13IMLGh*

My Fist for You

My fist is raised to defy oppression.
My head is bowed in reverence
for those who had the courage to endure.

I stand on this Olympic platform
in this moment of victory
for those who do not love me.

A win for those who sucked the dust
of hate, discrimination and violence
that I might live to honor them.

Here is my fist.

My Next Lifetime

In my next lifetime,
I want to be gifted
with a voice so powerful
that when I sing
you will bend your knees
and flood the earth with joyful tears.

You will look up at me
with those blue-green eyes
and watch me melt
in the arms of Spirit
from the power of your gaze.

I will sing from that place
deep in my heart reserved for you
over many lifetimes.

Do your thing tiger.
I will love you at a distance
on this sacred ground.

While my love for you
floats in eternity,
I will sing praise songs
in your name.

Season of Death

The army of death is all around us
lead by sacred souls wearing angel wings.
There is a long line at the rainbow bridge.
Lately it seems we come too often
to honor bonds to those who
touched our lives and massaged our hearts.

Death is part of the natural order but
comes so fast and takes so many
our heads swim in grief. We struggle
to process the sorrow squeezing the heart.
Many of us try to rub the pain of loss
from our foreheads as the whirlwind
of grief smacks hard against the planet.

I ask my Spiritual Guide, why are there so many?
I hear her in my head say, *this is the
cleansing wave*. All the souls leaving
the planet completed their cycle this time.
They go to rest, renew and prepare
for the next wave of rebirth.

The question is asked daily.
When will the season of healing begin?
After many days of contemplation,
I look up and see the healing light
in the distant horizon.

Ashok K. Bhargava

Ashok Bhargava is a poet, writer, community activist, public speaker, management consultant and a keen photographer. Based in Vancouver, he has published several collections of his poems: Riding the Tide, Mirror of Dreams, A Kernel of Truth, Skipping Stones, Half Open Door and Lost in the Morning Calm. His poetry has been published in various literary magazines and anthologies.

Ashok is a Poet Laureate and poet ambassador to Japan, Korea and India. He is founder of WIN: Writers International Network Canada. Its main objective is to inspire, encourage, promote and recognize writers of diverse genres, artists and community leaders. He has received many accolades including Nehru Humanitarian Award for his leadership of Writers International Network Canada, Poets without Borders Peace Award for his journeys across the globe to celebrate peace and to create alliances with poets, and Kalidasa Award for creative writings.

Fists Up

The silent shadows of self
become lightning rods

tender fingers slide together
resolute and determined

rise up as clenched fists
in the air

when denied
dignity and equality

in unity
in solidarity

at the same time
fully aware that

only with open hands
we can receive and give

Gravity of Fists

How many layers
of whiteness
has to be peeled

to discover
the reality that
black lives matter.

We have failed to sync
some of us
more than others.

Victims
of racism, injustice
and assault

know
the incidents and
what had happened to them

but afraid they are
to speak and
remain silent.

They can feel
their heart drumbeats
but refuse to hear it

before they become
clenched fists of resistance
of courage.

Heroes

Three men.
Luminous.
Determined.
Firm.

Two men with
Clenched fists
look down where
the earth and sky meet.

Third man
looks forward
for a horizon where
the sky and water meet.

Everyone
waiting for life's
changing scenes
changing expectations.

Sky and water covered
for now with clouds of gray
from where
a rainbow will appear.

Open eyes.
See the fists binding the air
the earth and the water
between us

while pain and pleasure
held together
open and fold
like powerful wings.

Caroline
'Ceri Naz'
Nazareno
Gabis

Carolin 'Ceri' Nazareno-Gabis

Caroline 'Ceri Naz' Nazareno-Gabis, author of Velvet Passions of Calibrated Quarks, World Poetry Canada International Director to Philippines is known as a 'poet of peace and friendship', a multi-awarded poet, editor, journalist, speaker, linguist, educator, peace and women's advocate. She believes that learning other's language and culture is a doorway to wisdom.

Among her poetic belts include PANORAMA YOUTH LITERARY AWARDS 2020, 7 th Prize Winner in the 19th, 20th and 21st Italian Award of Literary Festival; Writers International Network-Canada "Amazing Poet 2015", The Frang Bardhi Literary Prize 2014 (Albania), the sair-gazeteci or Poet Journalist Award 2014 (Tuzla, Istanbul, Turkey) and World Poetry Empowered Poet 2013 (Vancouver, Canada). She's a featured member of Association of Women's Rights and Development (AWID), The Poetry Posse, Galaktika Poetike, Asia Pacific Writers and Translators (APWT), Axlepino and Anacbanua.

Her poetry and children's stories have been featured in different anthologies and magazines worldwide.

Links to her works:

panitikan.ph/2018/03/30/caroline-nazareno-gabis

apwriters.org/author/ceri_naz/

www.aveviajera.org/nacionesunidasdelasletras/id1181.html

My color and the ocean of everything

I was born free
As free as the dark night
When silence have been burnt
Into mystic hums of emptiness,
I raise my hands and sing halleluia
And forever embrace my color
Black.
I am history
No matter what others say,
I have freed the white
To find me
In the light,
As you close your eyes
I am nothing,
But lend me some respect
For I know no reasons to kill
My bloodstream,
My life,
My will,
My song,
I am the ocean of everything,

I Can't Breathe

I can't breathe
I am trapped in your knees,
Facing down
I can feel your smoldering hands
Of bigotry,
I owe nothing.
Let me go.
I can't breathe
I am held down like a pauper,
Dragged to feel
The roughness of Minnesota street,
The right to live
In the land of the free
Is draining down
into darkness.
I am nothing.
Let me go.
I can't breathe.
I am breaking.
I fear that it's not free to shed a tear
My suffocated lungs can't sustain justice
This life has decayed for century of reasons
My fate has been detained
Into the abysmal mourning.
I am now free
To go.

A Prayer and Special Intention

Thank you Lord, for the borrowed life,
We entrust our lives to you,
Let your divine mercy
flow in each one of us,
You are the greatest cure
of all the illnesses in this land,
Protect us dear Father from the deadly viruses,
Calm our heart, mind and spirit
So we may help one another
To gather, cooperate and be healed as one,
Touch us now, Father,
Give us the good health that we need
In these trying times, bring us all closer to You,
Lord, You are our light, strength and power,
We believe, You are with us always and forever.
In Mighty Name of Jesus,
through the intercession of Mary our Mother

Swapna
Behera

Swapna Behera is a bilingual contemporary poet, author, translator and editor from Odisha, India. She was a teacher from 1984 to 2015. Her stories, poems and articles are widely published in National and International journals, and ezines, and are translated into different national and International languages. She has penned six books. She is the recipient of the Prestigious International Mother Language UGADI AWARD WINNER 2019. She was conferred upon the Prestigious International Poesis Award of Honor at the 2nd Bharat Award for Literature as Jury in 2015, The Enchanting Muse Award in India World Poetree Festival 2017, World Icon of Peace Award in 2017, and the Pentasi B World Fellow Poet in 2017. She is the recipient of the Prolific Poetess Award ,The Life time Achievement Award ,The Best Planner Award ,The Sahitya Shiromani Award, ATAL BIHARI BAJPAYEE Award, ATAL Award 2018 ,Global Literature Guardian Award ,International Life Time Achievement Award and the Master of Creative Impulse Award .She has received the Honoured Poet of India from the Seychelles Government accredited Literary Society Lasher one poem A NIGHT IN THE REFUGEE CAMP is translated into 60 languages .She is the Ambassador of Humanity by Hafrikan Prince Art World Africa 2018 and an official member of World Nation's Writers Union ,Kazakhstan2018. Italy, the National President for India by Hispanomundial Union of Writers (UHE), Peru, the administrator of several poetic groups, and the Cultural Ambassador for India and South Asia of Inner Child Press African is the life member of Odisha Environmental Society.

swapna.behera@gmail.com

a human rights salute that history remembers

a human rights salute
symbol of black power
the trio on the podium of medal ceremony
 two black-gloved clenched fists upraised
during the playing of the U.S. national anthem in the
Olympic
Smith and Carlos who won the gold and bronze
in two hundred metres Olympic
they stood on the podium with their human rights badge
 turning the face to the national flag
but the silver medallist Peter Norman ;
 a white athlete of par excellence
  wore the Olympic project badge for human rights
 in solidarity with them

the most overtly political statement
sympathetic was Norman to his competitors protest
suffered a lot in his own country Australia
Norman died setting a voice
 Smith and Carlos were the pall bearers at the funerals

after his death, the parliament
 begged apology to Norman
stating that was the moment of heroism and humility
an advanced international awareness for racial inequality
a silent gesture speaks so loud
louder is humility
than any voice
today ,tomorrow and forever.......

the lyrical investor

his lungs breathe
the punctuations, commas and finally the full stops
he is an investor
of his infant steps
perhaps
it is not easy for him to burn and fulfil his libidos
his songs echo in every courtyard
and
on the national highways
he is the crowned prince
while he stamps on the ballot paper
he questions the Supreme king
innumerable queries on his existence
that are always dumped in the quarries
his eyes are reflections of the sky

he is the Tathagat but he never leaves his wife
his anger and frustrations are the documents of a
democratic country
lo and behold
he is none other than a common man
a lyrical investor
moving
around his own axis ;weaving his own anthem
sowing his own emblem

you know, he is the common man
like you and me ....

Tathagat – Tathagat is a Pali word for Gautam Buddha

my father's shawl

a teacher he was
on the day of his superannuation
with a rose bouquet
the shawl was wrapped to him by his boss
the enigmatic meeting ended

the next day he started
shouting at mother
" give me my lunch box
I will miss my bus"
mother was smiling with tears in eyes
" dear ,today you have no school"

my father said
"oh, yes you are correct
now for me every day is Sunday "
he sat right on the sofa looked towards the blue sky
folded the shawl and preserved in the almirah
 some days I have seen him patting the fibre
may be feeling the aura of his integrity
perhaps feeling the seconds, minutes and years

my father's shawl

today he is lying on the carpet
wrapping the same shawl
which he saved throughout
rather invested his whole beings
to rewrite his final scriptures on the fire ....

Albert 'Infinite' Carrasco

Albert "Infinite The Poet" Carrasco is an urban poet, mentor and public speaker.

Albert believes his experience of growing up in poverty, dealing with drugs and witnessing murder over and over were lessons learnt, in order to gain knowledge to teach. Albert's harsh reality and honesty is a powerfully packed punch delivered through rhyme. Infinite grew up in the east part of the Bronx and still resides there, so he knows many young men will follow the same dark path he followed looking for change. The life of crime should never be an option to being poor but it is, very often.

Infinite poetry @lulu.com

Alcarrasco2 on YouTube

Infinite the poet on reverbnation

Infinite Poetry

http://www.lulu.com/us/en/shop/al-infinite-carrasco/infinite-poetry/paperback/product-21040240.html

Emory Douglas

We've been oppressed for many years. Too long. Inequality and racism led to a lot of blood shed and tears. We stayed strong. Stolen land, slavery, famine and poverty. It's all wrong. Children taken from mothers and fathers, Fathers and mothers ripped apart from the grips Of sons and daughters, When life was at its hardest we survived off of, Hope, song and prayers. I know it's hard to digest, we always expected the worst, It was a traditional curse,

But we still while prayed for the best. It has gotten to the point where we were no longer going tolerate hydrant sprays, the acts of divide and conquer, hunger, women and man slaughter. We had to become one, a unit moving together to defeat our oppressors. We had to bring our fight to light, like the Black Panthers show of power while fighting for our rights..

Acoustic range

I recite poems with an acoustic range that reaches my guardian angels in heaven. It's a cold cold world, if I go to the cemetery and spit my forte of poetry I'll give shivers to skeletons. What I belt is heard and felt by the people listening to the piece at the present time and those that died in the street or in hospitals fightn flatlines. When it comes to this art form, I'm cross platformed. Hurt and pain fuels my fire but it's murdered sons that give me 24 hour solar power. They are the reasons I see the light and write. See I came up with the smartest and strongest and most are with God or in the yard. These youngens and new hustlers don't have a chance, the problem is that they'll still try, they'll repeat our story, jail and death minus the money. I say minus the money because they're going to jail and dying without seeing lucrative currency. Why? Because what they think is a new spot is an old block that's been hot. They're tryn to eat while inheriting heat. It's just a matter of time before they get some or before they stare at a tip of a slug thru the barrel of gun, get wet up and left for dead in the slums. Nowadays it's a slow flow and dudes are hungry, no dough, so it's blam blam, John Doe, a process of elimination for dead prez accumulation from trees, pills, her-ron and blow. The game never changes, it's just new faces and new drug and gun cases.

24 hours to live

If I had twenty four hours to live it'll be trouble, I'll stick up all traps I know that bubble, I'll call connections and tell em I'll buy two if they give me one on the arm, give it to my right hand man and ask him to flip it for my fam and tell em I left it for tuition when I'm gone. I'll jump in my whip, jet on the west side highway to the diamond district, after a few liks I'll be jettn back on the fdr with a frozen SUV headn to the bricks to make the safe house icy, half for the team and half for wifey to make sure she doesn't need shit from nobody. On the twenty second hour I'll be parlaying with friends and family members, on the twenty third Ill get my lawyer to contact the DA to tell em they have to let my twenty five, forty five and lifer homies go, I'll do a lying confession, I'll tell em "it was me that touched fulano" cause he owed dough, they won't get a day from Bellaco because tomorrow I won't be here, they won't know. Ill plead guilty no need to try me, by the time I get to the island I'll be history... But others will be free, I'll end their stint and drop dead while they're doing my fingerprints.

Eliza Segiet

Eliza Segiet: Master's Degree in Philosophy, completed postgraduate studies in Cultural Knowledge, Philosophy, Arts and Literature at Jagiellonian University. She is a member of The Association of Polish Writers and The NWNU - Union of Writers of the World.

Her poems *Questions* and *Sea of Mists* won the title of the International Publication of the Year 2017 and 2018 in Spillwords Press.

For her volume of *Magnetic People* she won a literary award of a *Golden Rose* named after Jaroslaw Zielinski (Poland 2019 r.). Her poem The *Sea of Mists* was chosen as one of the best one hundred poems of 2018 by International Poetry Press Publication Canada.

In Poet's Yearbook, as the author of *Sea of Mists*, she was awarded with the prestigious Elite Writer's Status Award as one of the best poets of 2019 (July 2019).

She was awarded *World Poetic Star Award* by World Nations Writers Union – the world's largest Writers' Union from Kazakhstan (August 2019).

In September 2019 she was 1st Place Laureate (Foreign Poetry category) – in Contest *Quando È la Vita ad Invitare* for poem *Be Yourself* (Italy).

Her poem *Order* from volume *Unpaired* was selected as one of the 100 best poems of 2019 in International Poetry Press Publications (Canada).

Nominated for the Pushcart Prize 2019.

Nominated for the iWoman Global Awards (2019).

Laureate Naji Naaman Literary Prize 2020.

Laureate International Award PARAGON OF HOPE (Canada, 2020).

Obtained certificate of appreciation from *Gujarat Sahitya Academy* and *Motivational Strips* for literary excellence par with global standards (2020).

Ambassador of Literature granted by *Motivational Strips*.

Author's works can be found in anthologies, separate books and literary magazines worldwide.

Backdrop
To Emory Douglas

To win,
to still run after freedom
and tolerance,
fight for freedom in diversity.

Time and space
is nothing but a flashy backdrop
for people,
to whom closer is
winning a medal
than regards and understanding.

translated Ula de B.

Apeiron

Oxygenated by the world
she looks for a space of peace,
apeiron of happiness,
silence
in which the sound of the sea
and seagulls are a testimony to life.
She looks for the sun.

The world around the Eden has already hidden.

Translated by Artur Komoter

Labyrinth

In the vortex of dance,
wandering in the labyrinth of time
she saw
the ephemerality of existence.
Today turns into yesterday
as in the Heraklite river
– fluid, smooth.
Although trees live longer than humans,
slouching between them
one can see the scattered dandelions.
And behind a tall wall of boxwood
there is everything
one cannot go back to.
Every ray of the sun
is a hope for existence,
even though
at some point it will
not allow for a gust of life.

Translated by Artur Komoter

William S. Peters Sr.

Bill's writing career spans a period of over 50 years. Being first Published in 1972, Bill has since went on to Author in excess of 50 additional Volumes of Poetry, Short Stories, etc., expressing his thoughts on matters of the Heart, Spirit, Consciousness and Humanity. His primary focus is that of Love, Peace and Understanding!

Bill says . . .

I have always likened Life to that of a Garden. So, for me, Life is simply about the Seeds we Sow and Nourish. All things we "Think and Do", will "Be" Cause and eventually manifest itself to being an "Effect" within our own personal "Existences" and "Experiences" . . . whether it be Fruit, Flowers, Weeds or Barren Landscapes! Bill highly regards the Fruits of his Labor and wishes that everyone would thus go on to plant "Lovely" Seeds on "Good Ground" in their own Gardens of Life!

to connect with Bill, he is all things Inner Child

www.iaminnerchild.com

Personal Web Site

www.iamjustbill.com

1968 . . . Yes We Can!!!

We earned it,
We won the race,
We placed 1 & 2 . . .
First and Second
In the race of our lives
We won,
But we lost

On the stage of our lives
We put it all
On the line
To let the world know
Of our struggle . . .
As a people

The powers to be
Did not wish to acknowledge
Such an ugliness,
For denial was the soup
Being served

The media,
The overtly sensationalized media
Condemned us
Just as they condemned any
Efforts and retorts
Of the oppressed
To get that damn boot
Or knee
Off of our necks

Though our efforts
Were marginalized
Minimalized
And vilified,

.....
History will not lie
About what we have been through,
Are still yet going through
In the attempt
For parity,
Justice,
Equality,
And an opportunity
To show that
Yes we can!

The Keeper

I am not the keeper of your Castle,
I am the Keeper of your Dreams

I just thought I would remind you
Of this,
For it seems
That you have forgotten
Our pact

The fact is,
We have committed to love,
One and another,
A love that is destined
To travel across
The endless streams
Of time
And of course
Our Dreams

You are the key
To my fantasies,
My realities
And the ship
That carries me across
All the seas
Of all existence

The consistence is evident,
A certifiable providence
That fills my soul,
Mends all holes
That I once had
In this heart of mine

The handwriting was on the wall
The call signs were blushingly dancing
Within the spirit
Of all that I am,
All that I thought I was,
And thus
All that I can ever be

And I have to let you know
That . . .
You are the keeper of my Castle,
You are the Keeper of my Dreams.

And the flowers sang . . .

Laughter and Sarcasm

I ask you . . .
What would life be
Without a little
Laughter and sarcasm?

My God, that would be horrible,
And perhaps painful and gloomy
With no room for the assholes
To escape . . . including myself
…..
Melancholy?

Anger and Anger Management
Would be 'off the charts'
What a good business
To be in . . . huh?

I wonder would there finally be parity
In the prison population,
Where the sensation of justice
Is no longer 'just-us'
And a few others
Who do not fit in.
…..
And what about economics
And all the other BS that fills our lives
With inequities

I laugh at many things
That otherwise would give cause
For me to react,
Or learn to be indifferent,
Like so many others.

Unfortunately,
Mothers can not escape
The waves of responsibility
For their children
Who happen to be on an errant path,
Or just caught up
In the wrong shit,
At the wrong time . . .
Be it their guilt . . .
Or not

These days
My sense of humor,
Many times,
Makes no sense,
For it vilifies me
By way of my own
'dumb-downed-ness'
Which I have somehow voluntarily
Acquiesced to

. . .
GO Figure

There seems to be
So much to laugh at
These days . . .
From Religion to Politics
To the greed of the elitists
And 'others' who attempt
To emulate
Their demented ways.

We follow the lines of conformance,
Right over the cliff,

Like the non-thinking
Swine that humanity has become,
In certain definable demographics

I guess we all need something
To believe in,
But some of the rhetoric and propaganda
We are willing to embrace,
I can only laugh at,
As I laugh at myself as well

We spend time,
Telling ourselves
That life needs to be fixed,
Without ever asserting any cause
To self
For the fixing

How can I ascertain
What is wrong with the world,
Or when are we going to change
Without first looking at myself . . .
. . . .
Judgement
That's a killer,
Isn't it?

When I ponder some of the aspects
Of what I am capable of noticing,
I most times am susceptible
To becoming
Soulfully convoluted,
Polluted,
And self-disputing,

And as thus stated
In this humble offering
Some may attribute as poetry,
I realize
There is something rotten
In the demise of our humanity
Where sanity and integrity becomes an
Unsought attribute
As we give tribute
To the craziness
Of conspiracy and complacency
…..
So what is left I ask you
Save Laughter and Sarcasm

This has been my perspective
Of what is wrong with me . . .
How about you?

William S. Peters, Sr.

February
2021
Featured Poets

~ * ~

T.Ramesh Babu

Ruchida Barman

Neptune Barman

Faleeha Hassan

i FLY because I Can

...said the Dreamer to the world.

www.iamjustbill.com

T.
Ramesh
Babu

Dr.T.Ramesh Babu working as Assistant Professor (Ad-hoc) in the department of Humanities & Social Sciences, JNTUA CEP, Pulivendula, YSR KADAPA Dist. Andhra Pradesh, India. He is a poet, writer, author, professional teacher and soft skills trainer. He was born on 6th January 1981 in Guntakal, Anantapur Dist. He received his highest degree Ph.D. from Acharya Nagarjuna University, Guntur, Andhra Pradesh in 2017. He has published 16 International & 2 National papers. He is author of 03 international books 02 published with LAP LAMBERT Publishers and 01 published with HSRA Bangalore with collection of 35 poems. Many poems have been published in international anthologies and magazines too.

Moring View in Woods

The blue night sky fades
As lighter blue streaks in sky
Cacophony sings
A dawn chorus as
Thrushes, black-birds, robins, goldfinches
The morning singers
Making resonant
Sweet chirping sounds relaxing
The mood of nature
As pleasant as paradise
Slanting sunbeams flickering
Through foliage in woods
The fresh breath of wind
Reverberating in woods
With a melody
The nature is so
Amazing one in pleasure
Sharing on the Earth.

Waiting for....

The black flat dry lands;
Opened their mouths and,
Splintered with enormous thirst
Your arrival may be quenched.

All the wild beasts and birds;
Tracing and exploring for a stream or,
A lake in woods, but they runoff,
The wild life looks at sky with a ray of hope.

The swollen rivers quieten,
The brimming streams evacuated,
The running brooklets dawdled,
Now they all bide their time to recommence.

Look at all these desperate,
Downpour your blessings;
As cloudburst to fill cheeriness;

My Pure Love

I don't know what it is
Called people may call it
Love but, to me it is an emotional
Feeling and an invisible bonding
Between you and me, I won't say that it is
Infatuation because, my feelings are not
Short-time on you, whether you are with me
Or not I admire you forever I always try to
Like a wave in the sea to reach seashore
Though the wave won't be with seashore but
It touches similarly I may not be with you,
But your thoughts with me forever the
Wonderful moments which we had together
Together were ceased and hark back
Those moments and respiring
Throughout life as Chakor
Partridge love for moon,
I'll be waiting for you
As pied crested
Cuckoo waits for
Rain I'll be for
You until
My last
Breathe.

Ruchida
Barman

Dr. Ruchida Barman is a Professor in English. She currently is working in JECRC, Sitapura in the Department of English and Humanities. She has a total experience of 27 years of teaching out of which 17 are at the undergraduate level. Dr. Barman says . . . I have a variety of facets to my personality. Teaching is not just a profession for me it is my passion. I am a creative writer too who writes poetry, as well as articles. I am also a soft skill trainer.

Nature

I saw the rain drops falling
Sitting on the window sill
I thought the nature was crying
Just as I was.

I saw the rain drops falling
Sitting on the swing
I thought the nature was rejoicing
Just as I was.

I saw the clouds in the sky
Looking from my window
I thought the nature was feeling low
Just as I was

I saw the clouds in the sky
Looking up from my garden
I thought the nature was happy
Just as I was

I realized then, Nature is our best friend
Standing by us always
Reflecting our moods and emotions
Just as we do

Separation

I separated from you-body, mind and soul
I separated from you complete and whole
It was inevitable, It was sure
It had to happen I was sure.
I had to do this to keep my self – respect
Or else there would be scar on my aspect
My inner self was hurt, I was choked.
I had to breathe, if I had to live.
When the point came to choose between living and
suffocating,
I chose to live.
My decision was simple and clear,
You and I were never near

When she was born

All said she was lucky
She would be the loved one always
She would be the blessed one always

She was pampered and loved
She was blessed
As she grew she realized she was lucky
To have a loving family

She loved her Parents,
She loved her Sibling,
She loved her friends,
She loved her self,

AND then the beautiful world crashed,
SHE GOT MARRIED
She got estranged from her Parents,
She got estranged from her sibling
She got estranged from her friends
AND got estranged from HERSELF

The only gift that helped her to live
Was her little angel with broken wings
She gave her the reason to live
She gave her the song to sing

AND then God suddenly took pity on her
He gave her another angel
Who understood her silence
Who understood all her silent sufferings
She now wanted to live
LIVE for herself, LIVE to be happy,
LIVE to be loved, Live to be understood

She knew she found her soulmate
She knew she found her love
She was thankful to God
She was thankful to her angel

All the pain of her life vanished
All the trouble vanished
With a little gesture
With a little word
HE GAVE HER LIFE BACK TO HER

Ruchida Barman

Neptune
Barman

I am Neptune Barman staying in Delhi, India. I am doing graduation in English honors in Delhi University. I love to travel and express my feelings of heart in form of poetry. I have self-published 2 books on poetry and 1 book on my life recently. I have been writing poetry since i was 12 years old. Poetry for me is language of heart that can connect the humanity and make a better tomorrow.

Silent Tears

Each day passes like the day before
but night is never the same
when the world goes silent
my heart speaks alone
screaming without a sound
lie in a corner unknown to the world
the heart turns heavy like the clouds in the sky
and drops of prayer slides down my cheek
making me helpless all the night
sometime the strongest in morning are to cry all night
this tears in me not my weakness
but existence of love and pain in my heart
if these tears could build a way to heaven
I would walk alone to bring you back
though an ocean I cried
but am thankful to those tears
because our love has never died

Behind the Line

To any reader of my poem
Look through the window
Hidden behind these line
Remember to hold these lines
Carefully in your heart
As it's ageing with time
But don`t follow my line
Because these lines are fake
With a fake smile on its face
Just to entertain you
Until it's time to complete performance
Behind these line lies a window
Which I never dared to go through
There lies the memories
That grew as a knife in my life
And it hurts me each time I want to fly
Rivers of tears that flowed
Shall meet ocean so far
But this broken heart still beats
Like the stars shining in the sky

Mother's Letter to her son

Oh my son of my womb
am ashamed to call you my son
i cried each night in dark
when you were in my womb
cried for you to meet my poverty
escaped you 9 months from rest world
but lost you the day saw your face
leaving behind barren soul in me
your twin brother too young
your mother's too poor
I tried death but stopped
looking your brother cries
am sorry my dear son
to leave you from my eyes
to sell you to feed your brother
to let you live a life of my dream
a life i could`not give you
and let your brother too
I dream each night of you
your presence beside me
even know you could never be mine
you got better mother
a life of joy, a life of dream
that i could never afford my son
But have a dream to see you like star
Shining in the night sky
And live my life with few tears in smile

Faleeha Hassan

Faleeha Hassan, is a poet, teacher, editor, writer, playwriter from Iraq, who now lives in the USA. She is the first woman to write poetry for children in Iraq. She received master's degree in Arabic literature, and has published 24 books. Her poems have been translated into 15 languages. Her book, *Breakfast for Butterflies* was nominated for the 2018 Pulitzer Prize. Ms. Hassan also serves as an Cultural Ambassador - Iraq, USA for Inner Child Press International.

You want me to forget you?

Easy

Force my eyes to look at things without seeing the sparkle

of your smile

Wipe from my hair the tenderness of your touch

Remove the warmth of your hugs from my cold arms

Teach your name not to slip from my tongue when I speak

to someone else

Yes,

Find another beat for my heart

And I will disappear like a snowflake when it touches

warm ground

The art of my transformation

Who is she?
Is this me?
The girl who was so beautiful
Two seconds ago
Like a fact
Coming from the mouth of an innocent child
playful as the warmth of a flame
from a charcoal stove on winter nights
Is this me?
Really?
So, who dug these grooves on my forehead?
Who stole the glimmer of my face
And replaced it with of spots of ash?
Whose puffs those bags under my eyes
And fills them with sadness and worry?
Since when was the softness of my cheeks replaced with
two sharp bones?
I need strong fingers to lift sides of my mouth
And very strong reason to smile.
Even if I did this
There is nothing Just an abandoned cave that has no lustre.
Why do these barbed wires grow in my nostrils?
Wow
Now I realize
Time is an incredible cartoonist.

No one said London is very cold!

Because I only sailed in the warmth of my city
And I never shook a snowman's hand
I didn't notice the wool socks or leather gloves
And because quoting is forbidden – in my mom's opinion -
I did not borrow a coat from Gogol *
Or anyone else
 I packed a bundle of my hot memories
And I left
....
The loving hearts shortened my farewell with fast beats
And reduced all their wishes to one "stay warm"
But before I could blink
Her watch came close to me
Shouted in my ear -: Big Ben*
I was terrified
When my stories froze.
The watch fell on her back laughing
When I told her:
 I was hiding in the pocket of my poem
 Warming by the fabric of letters.

....
*Gogol is the Russian novelist Nikolai Gogol, author of the
coat story that novelist Turgenev said, "We all got out of
Gogol's coat."

*Big Ben is the famous London clock that started in 1859

Remembering

our fallen soldiers of verse

Janet Perkins Caldwell

February 14, 1959 ~ September 20, 2016

Alan W. Jankowski

16 March 1961 ~ 10 March 2017

Now available

World Healing World Peace
2020

Poets for Humanity

Inner Child Press

News

Poetry Posse Members

We are so excited to share and announce a few of the current books, as well as the new and upcoming books of some of our Poetry Posse authors.

On the following pages we present to you ...

Jackie Davis Allen

Gail Weston Shazor

hülya n. yılmaz

Nizar Sartawi

Faleeha Hassan

Fahredin Shehu

Caroline 'Ceri' Nazareno

Eliza Segiet

Teresa E. Gallion

William S. Peters, Sr.

COMING SOON
www.innerchildpress.com

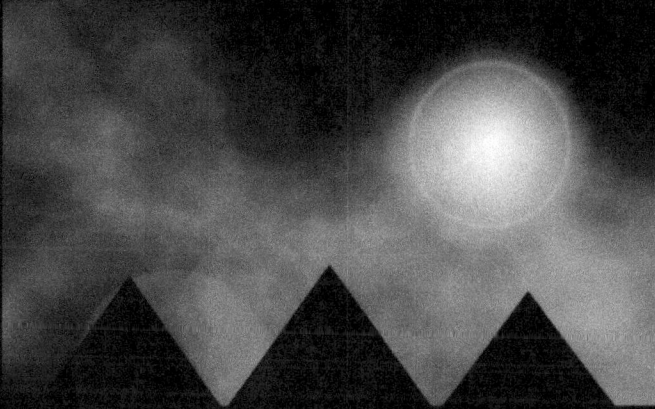

Eliza Segiet

To Be More

Now Available at
www.innerchildpress.com

Scent of Love

Poetry by

Teresa E. Gallion

Now Available

www.innerchildpress.com

Now Available

www.innerchildpress.com

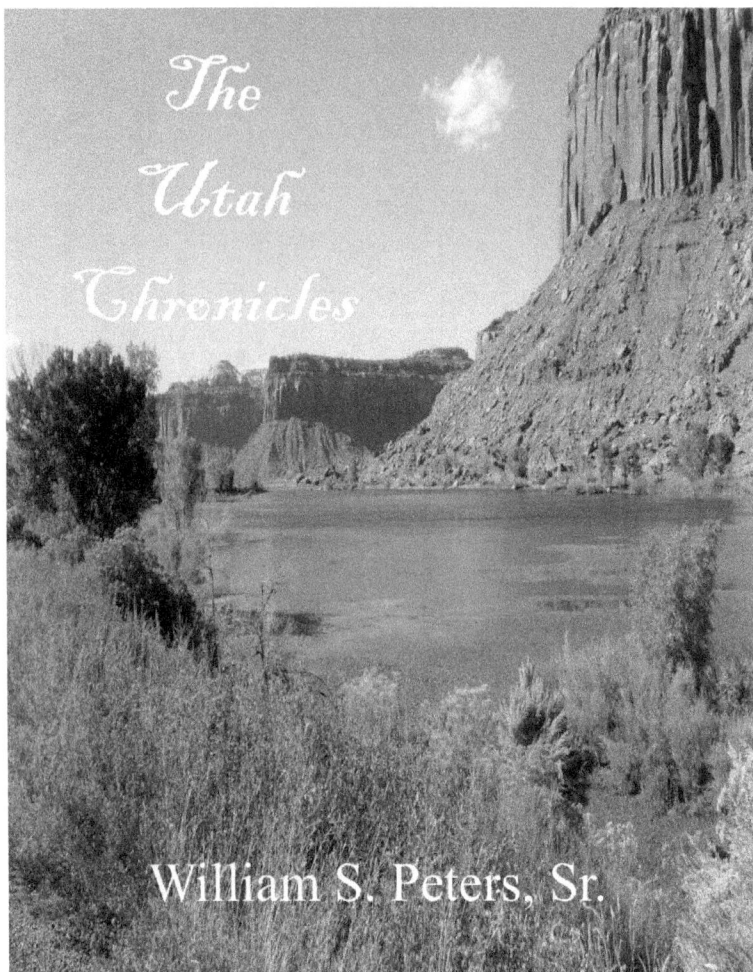

The
Utah
Chronicles

William S. Peters, Sr.

Now Available

www.innerchildpress.com

One Eye Open

u n i r 1.

william s. peters, sr

COMING SOON

<u>*www.innerchildpress.com*</u>

The Book of krisar

volume v

william s. peters, sr.

Now Available

www.innerchildpress.com

The Book of krisar

Volume I

william s. peters, sr.

The Book of krisar

Volume II

william s. peters, sr.

Now Available

www.innerchildpress.com

The Book of krisar

Volume III

william s. peters, sr.

The Book of krisar

Volume IV

william s. peters, sr.

Now Available

www.innerchildpress.com

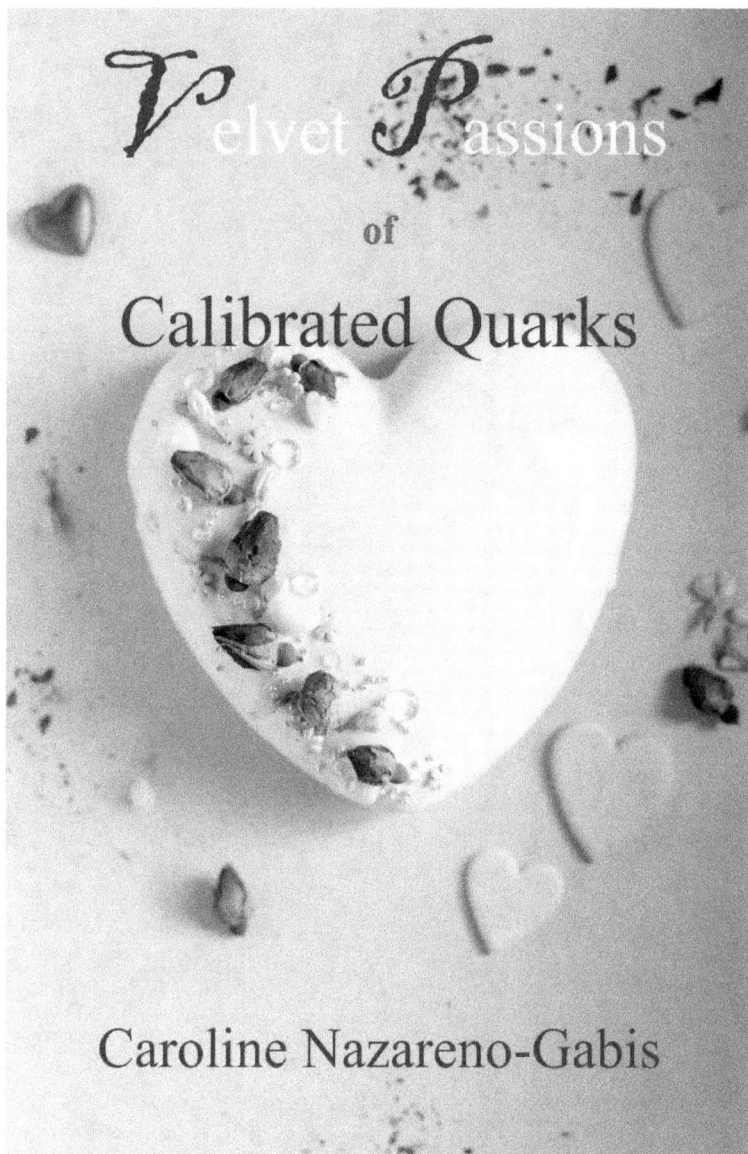

Velvet Passions

of

Calibrated Quarks

Caroline Nazareno-Gabis

Inner Child Press News

Now Available

www.innerchildpress.com

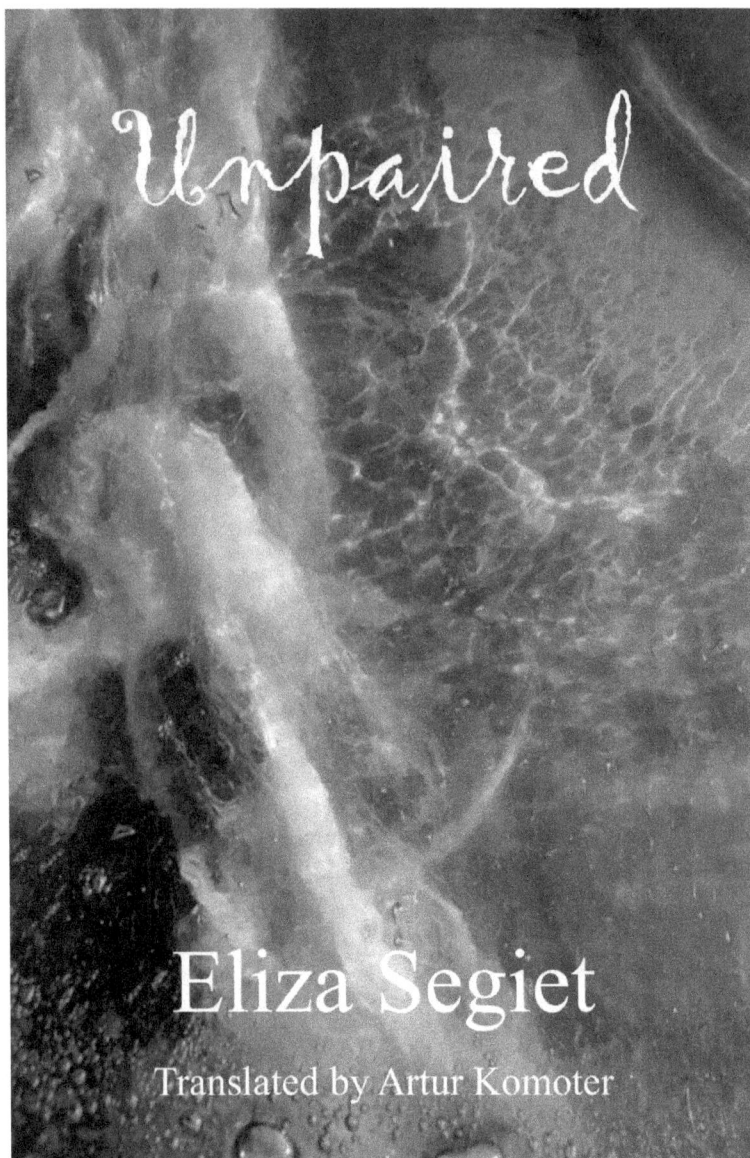

Unpaired

Eliza Segiet

Translated by Artur Komoter

Private Issue

www.innerchildpress.com

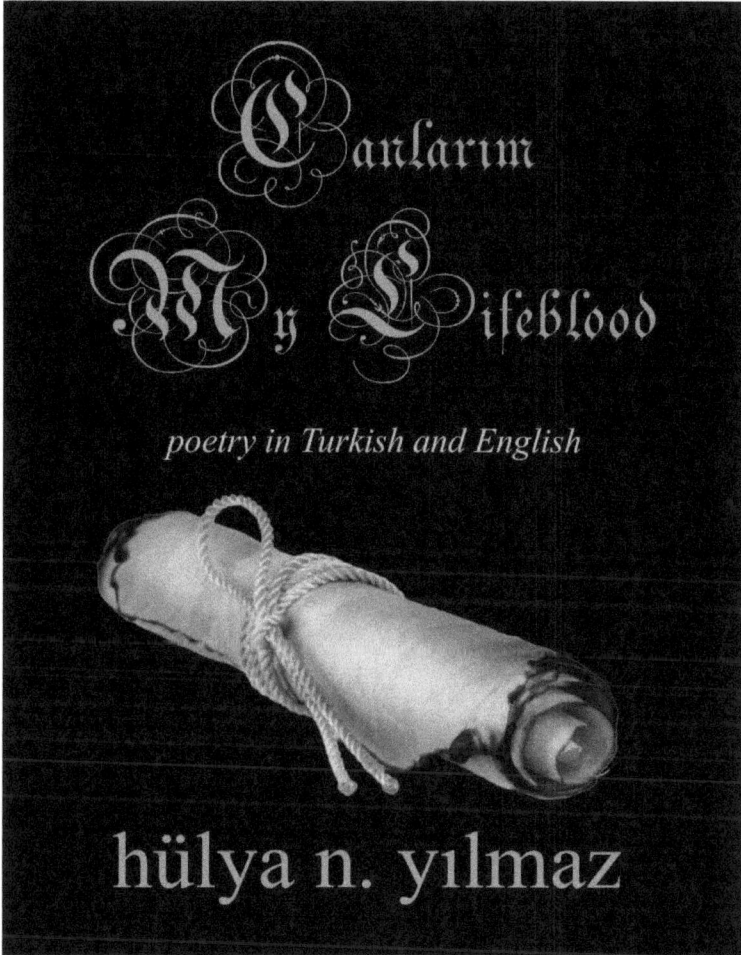

Canlarım
My Lifeblood

poetry in Turkish and English

hülya n. yılmaz

Now Available

www.innerchildpress.com

Butterfly's Voice

Faleeha Hassan

Translated by William M. Hutchins

Now Available at
www.innerchildpress.com

No Illusions

Through the Looking Glass

Jackie Davis Allen

Now Available at
www.innerchildpress.com

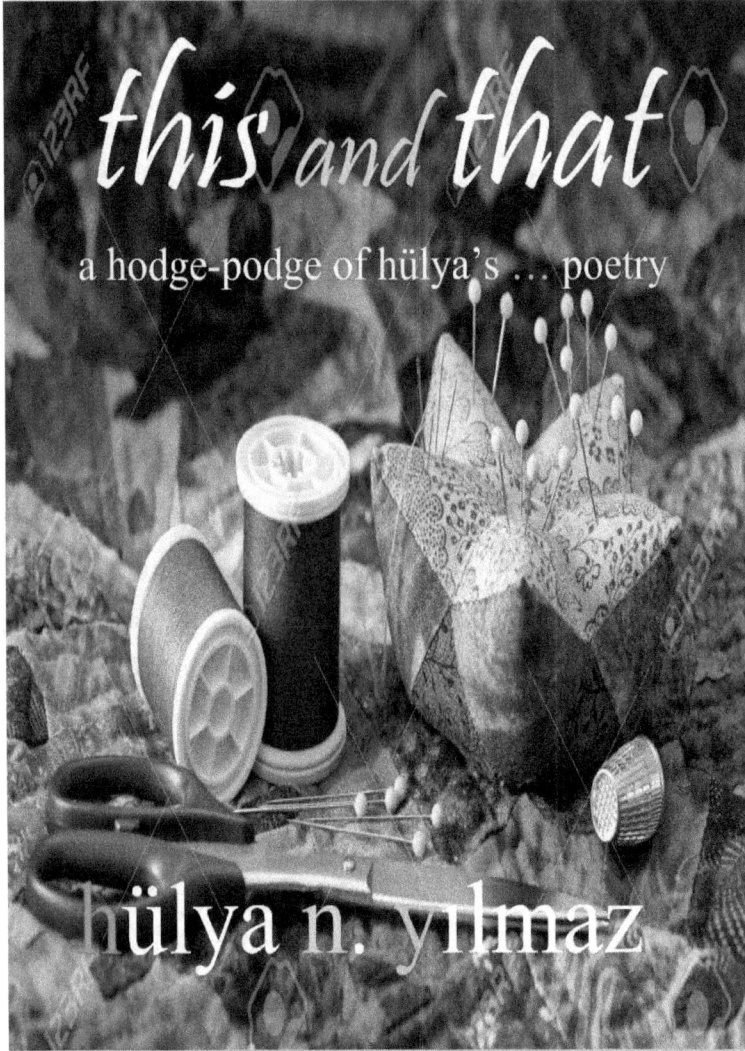

this and that

a hodge-podge of hülya's ... poetry

hülya n. yılmaz

Now Available at

www.innerchildpress.com

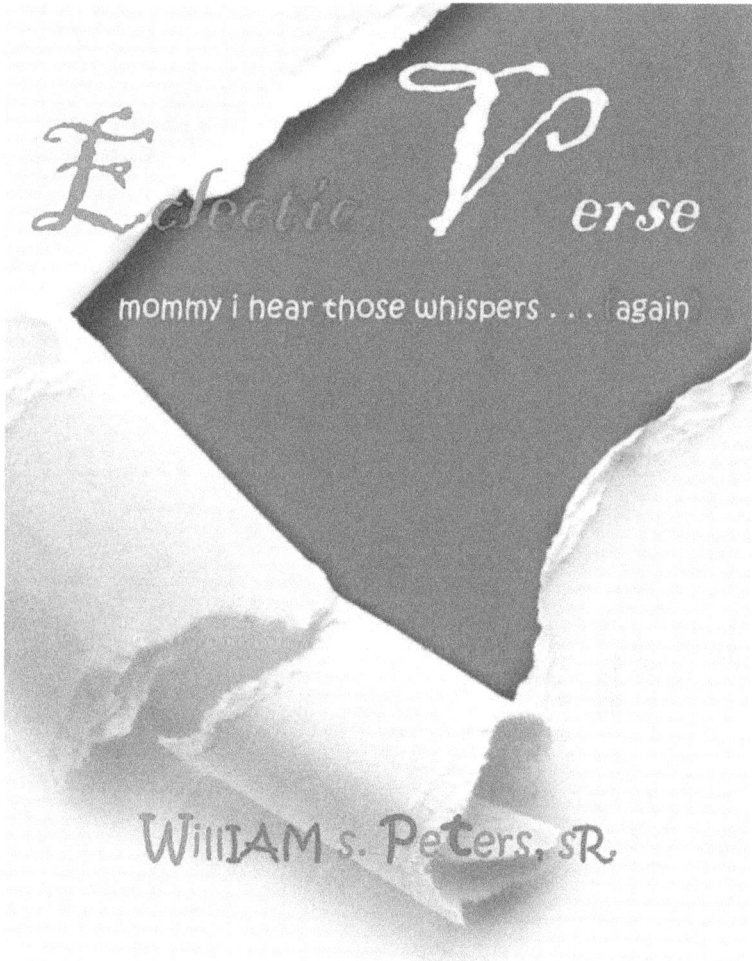

Inner Child Press News

Now Available at
www.innerchildpress.com

HERENOW

FAHREDIN SHEHU

Now Available at
www.innerchildpress.com

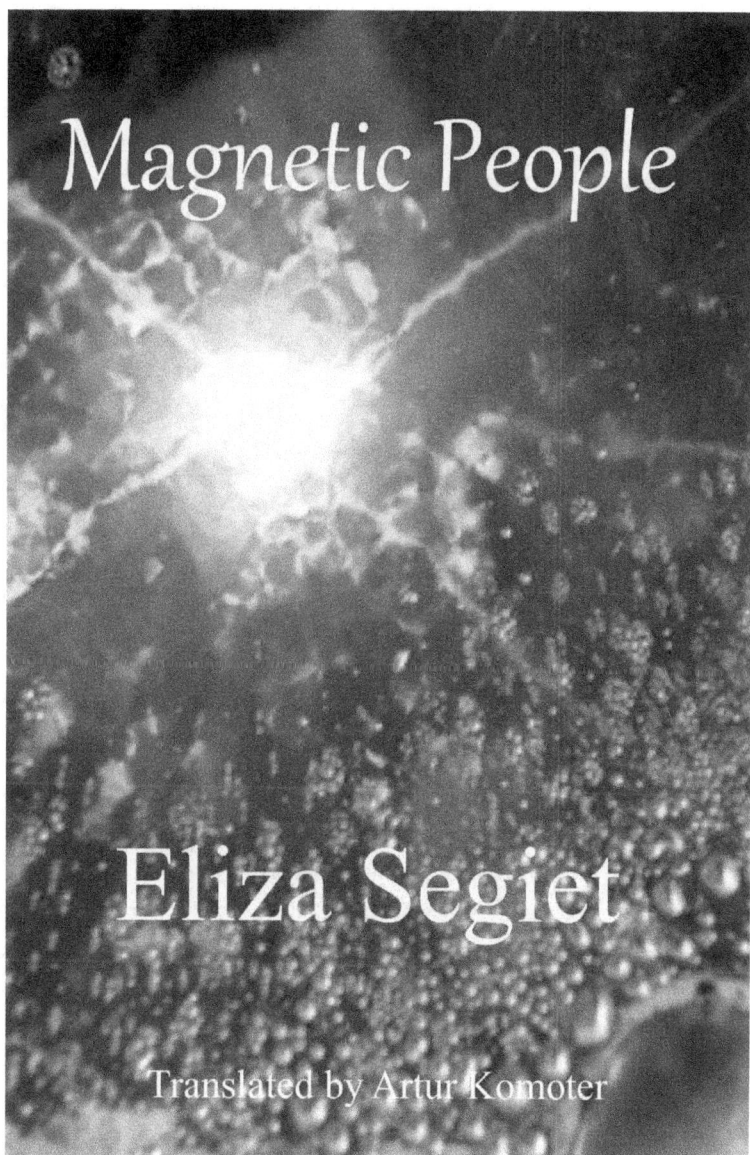

Magnetic People

Eliza Segiet

Translated by Artur Komoter

Now Available at

www.innerchildpress.com

Dark Side

of the

Moon

Jackie Davis Allen

Now Available at
www.innerchildpress.com

Lies My Grandfathers Told Me

Gail Weston Shazor

Aflame

Memoirs in Verse

hülya n. yılmaz

Now Available at

www.innerchildpress.com

Mass Graves

Faleeha Hassan

Inner Child Press News

Now Available at
www.innerchildpress.com

Breakfast

for

Butterflies

Faleeha Hassan

Now Available at

www.innerchildpress.com

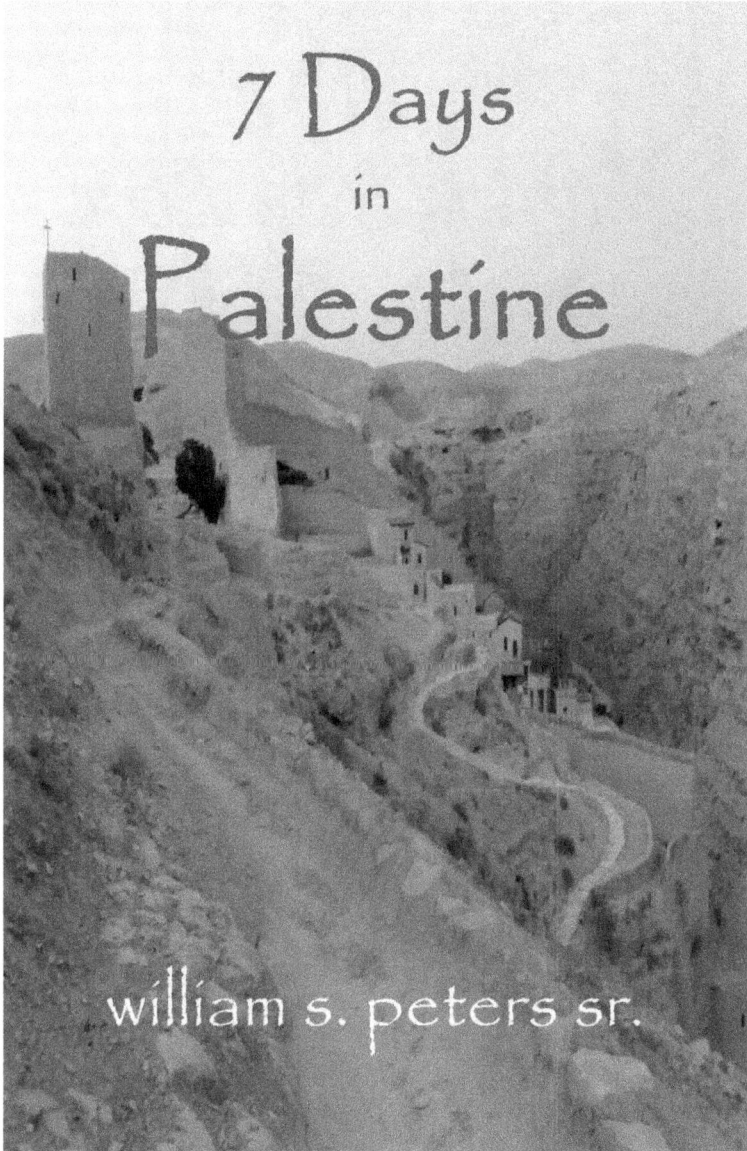

7 Days
in
Palestine

william s. peters sr.

Now Available at
www.innerchildpress.com

inner child press
presents

Tunisia My Love

william s. peters, sr.

Now Available at

www.innerchildpress.com

INNER CHILD PRESS

THIS IS WHY I
SLEEP

william s. peters sr.

Now Available at
www.innerchildpress.com

Inward Reflections

Think on These Things
Book II

william s. peters, sr.

Other

Anthological

works from

Inner Child Press International

www.innerchildpress.com

World Healing World Peace
2020

Poets for Humanity

Now Available

www.worldhealingworldpeacepoetry.com

Now Available

www.innerchildpress.com

Inner Child Press International
&
The Year of the Poet
present

Poetry

the best of 2020

Poets of the World

Now Available
www.innerchildpress.com

Inner Child Press International

presents

W.A.R.

We Are Revolution

Poets for Humanity

Now Available
www.innerchildpress.com

the **H**eart of a **P**oet

words for a better tomorrow

The Conscious Poets

Now Available
www.innerchildpress.com

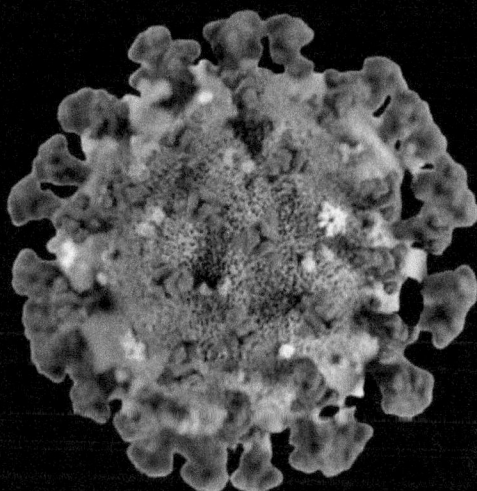

Corona

Social Distancing

Poets for Humanity

Now Available

www.innerchildpress.com

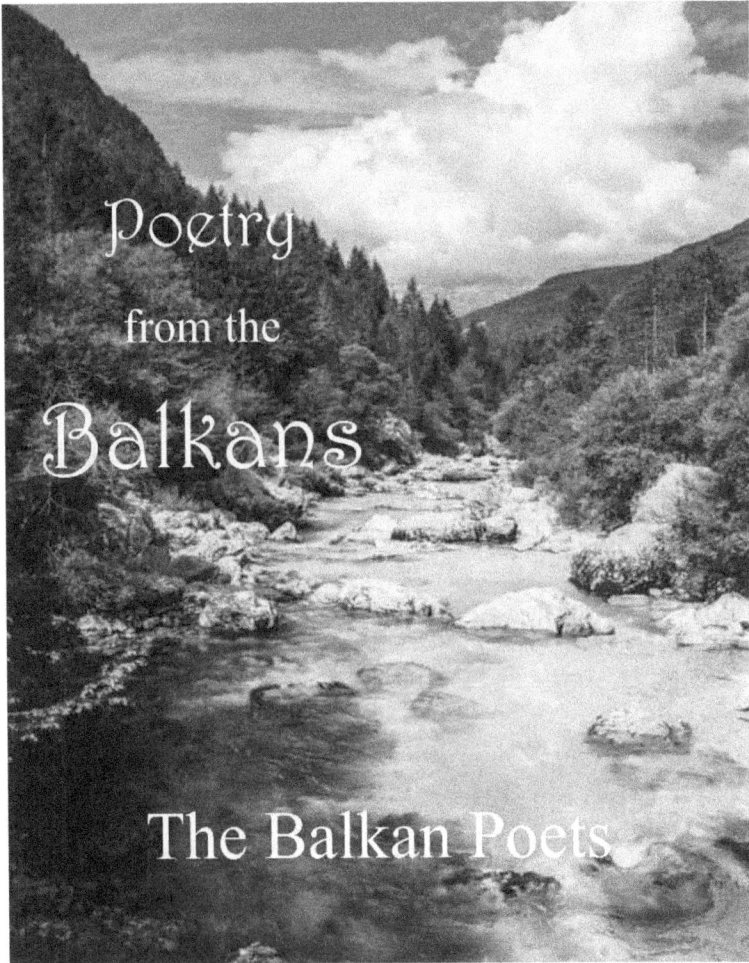

Poetry from the Balkans

The Balkan Poets

Now Available at
www.innerchildpress.com

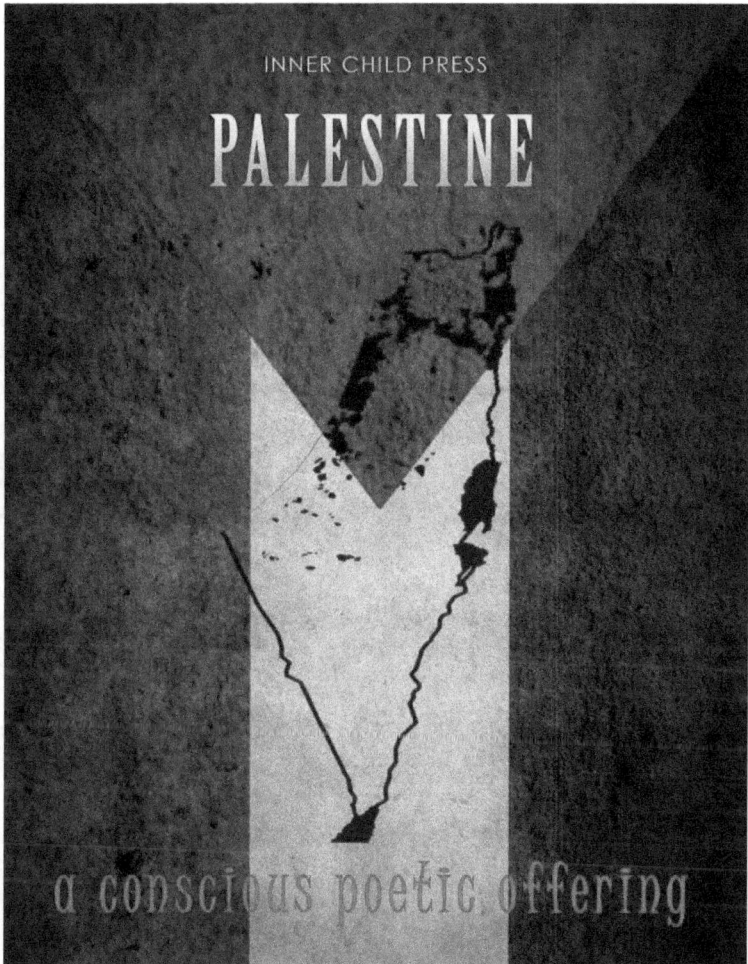

INNER CHILD PRESS

PALESTINE

a conscious poetic offering

Now Available at
www.innerchildpress.com

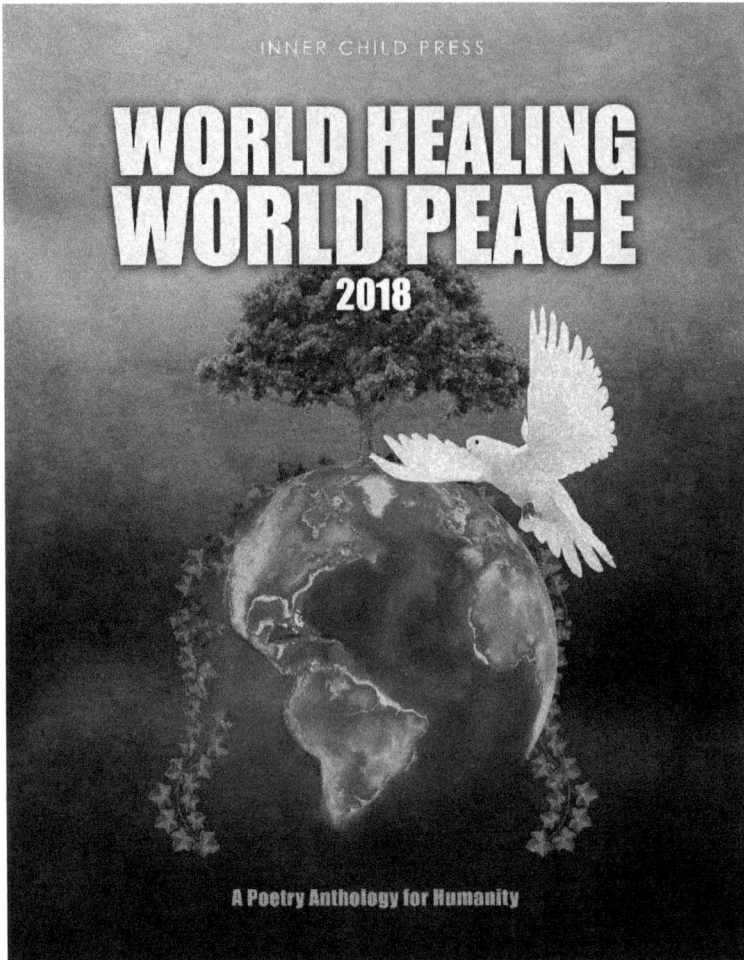

Now Available at
www.innerchildpress.com

Inner Child Press International
presents

A Love Anthology

2019

The Love Poets

Now Available

www.worldhealingworldpeacepoetry.com

Now Available

www.worldhealingworldpeacepoetry.com

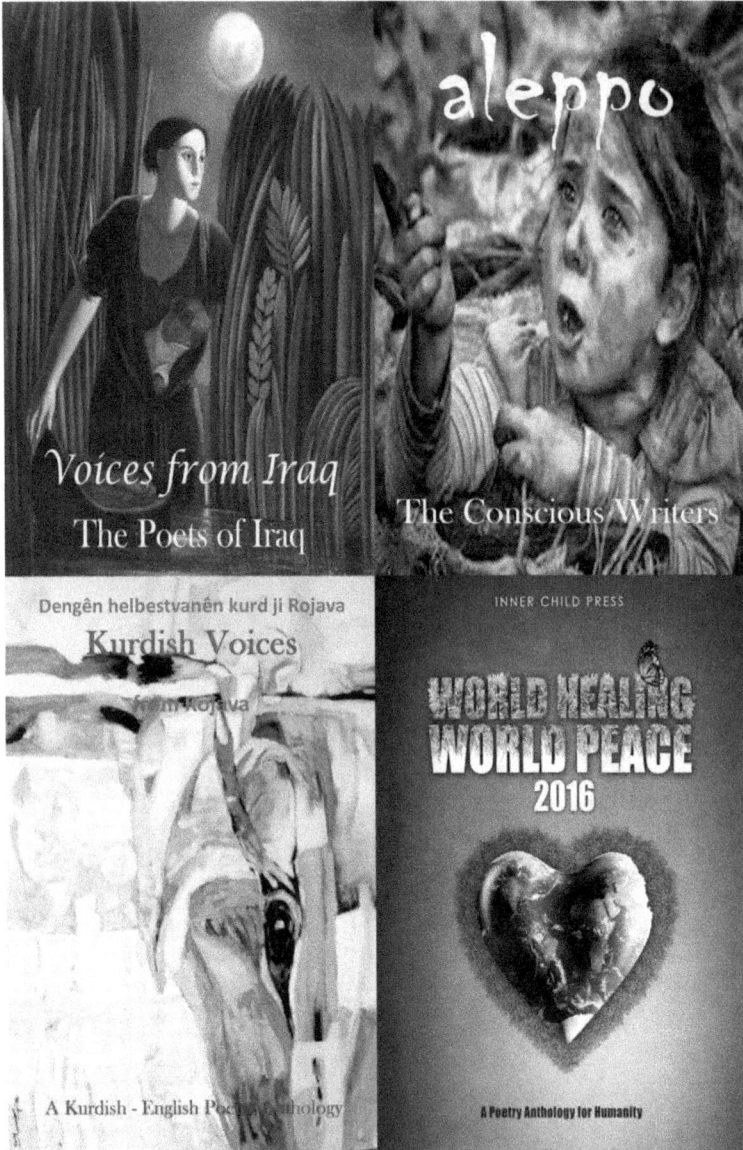

Now Available

www.innerchildpress.com/anthologies

Mandela

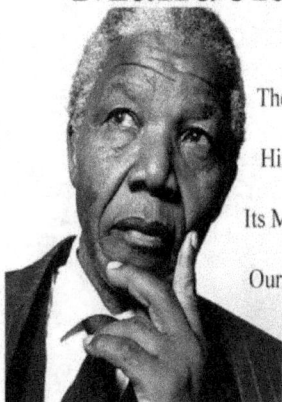

The Man

His Life

Its Meaning

Our Words

Poetry . . . Commentary & Stories
The Anthological Writers

A GATHERING OF WORDS

POETRY & COMMENTARY
FOR
TRAYVON MARTIN

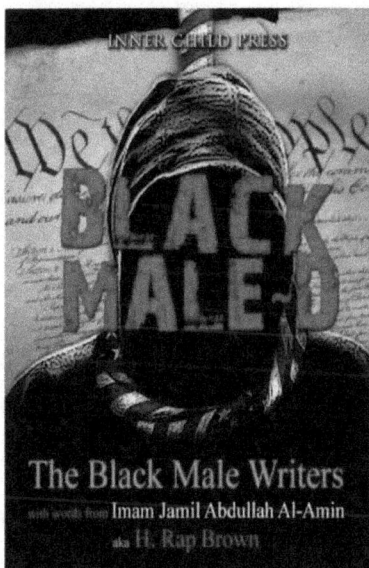

INNER CHILD PRESS

BLACK MALE-D

The Black Male Writers
with words from Imam Jamil Abdullah Al-Amin
aka H. Rap Brown

I
want
my
poetry
to... *volume* 4

the conscious poets
inspired by . . . Monte Smith

Now Available

www.innerchildpress.com/anthologies

Now Available

www.innerchildpress.com/anthologies

Janet
gone too soon . . .

healing through words

Poetry ... Prose ... Prayer ... Stories

a
Poetically
Spoken
Anthology
volume 1
Collector's Edition

The Poetry Posse
Presents

an anthology
of

Love

The Poetry Posse 2016

Now Available

www.innerchildpress.com/anthologies

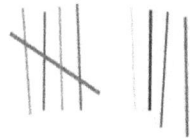

Now Available

www.innerchildpress.com/anthologies

The Year of the Poet
January 2014

The Poetry Posse

Jamie Bond
Gail Weston Shazor
Albert 'Infinite' Carrasco
Siddartha Beth Pierce
Janet P. Caldwell
June 'Bugg' Barefield
Debbie M. Allen
Tony Henninger
Joe DaVerbal Minddancer
Robert Gibbons
Neetu Wali
Shareef Abdur-Rasheed
William S. Peters, Sr.

Carnation

Our January Feature
Terri L. Johnson

the Year of the Poet
February 2014

violets

The Poetry Posse

Jamie Bond
Gail Weston Shazor
Albert 'Infinite' Carrasco
Siddartha Beth Pierce
Janet P. Caldwell
June 'Bugg' Barefield
Debbie M. Allen
Tony Henninger
Joe DaVerbal Minddancer
Robert Gibbons
Neetu Wali
Shareef Abdur-Rasheed
William S. Peters, Sr.

Our February Features
Teresa E. Gallion & Robert Gibson

the Year of the Poet
March 2014

The Poetry Posse

Jamie Bond
Gail Weston Shazor
Albert 'Infinite' Carrasco
Siddartha Beth Pierce
Janet P. Caldwell
June 'Bugg' Barefield
Debbie M. Allen
Tony Henninger
Joe DaVerbal Minddancer
Robert Gibbons
Neetu Wali
Shareef Abdur-Rasheed
Kimberly Burnham
William S. Peters, Sr.

daffodil

Our March Featured Poets
Alicia C. Cooper & hülya yılmaz

the Year of the Poet
April 2014

The Poetry Posse

Jamie Bond
Gail Weston Shazor
Albert 'Infinite' Carrasco
Siddartha Beth Pierce
Janet P. Caldwell
June 'Bugg' Barefield
Debbie M. Allen
Tony Henninger
Joe DaVerbal Minddancer
Robert Gibbons
Neetu Wali
Shareef Abdur-Rasheed
Kimberly Burnham
William S. Peters, Sr.

Our April Featured Poets
Fahredin Shehu
Martina Reisz Newberry
Justin Blackburn
Monte Smith

Sweet Pea

celebrating international poetry month

Now Available

www.innerchildpress.com/the-year-of-the-poet

185

Inner Child Press Anthologies

The Year of the Poet
September 2014

Aster   Morning-Glory

Wild Cranberry September Birth of Flower

September Feature Poets
Florence Malone * Keith Alan Hamilton

The Poetry Posse
Jamie Bond * Gail Weston Shazor * Albert 'Infinite' Carrasco * Siddartha Beth Pierce
Janet P. Caldwell * June 'Bugg' Barefield * Debbie M. Allen * Tony Henninger
Joe DaVerbal Minddancer * Robert Gibbons * Neetu Wali * Shareef Abdur-Rasheed
Kimberly Burnham * William S. Peters, Sr.

THE YEAR OF THE POET
October 2014

Red Poppy

The Poetry Posse
Jamie Bond * Gail Weston Shazor * Albert 'Infinite' Carrasco * Siddartha Beth Pierce
Janet P. Caldwell * June 'Bugg' Barefield * Debbie M. Allen * Tony Henninger
Joe DaVerbal Minddancer * Robert Gibbons * Neetu Wali * Shareef Abdur-Rasheed
Kimberly Burnham * William S. Peters, Sr.

October Feature Poets
Ceri Naz * Rajendra Padhi * Elizabeth Castillo

THE YEAR OF THE POET
November 2014

Chrysanthemum

The Poetry Posse
Jamie Bond * Gail Weston Shazor * Albert 'Infinite' Carrasco * Siddartha Beth Pierce
Janet P. Caldwell * June 'Bugg' Barefield * Debbie M. Allen * Tony Henninger
Joe DaVerbal Minddancer * Robert Gibbons * Neetu Wali * Shareef Abdur-Rasheed
Kimberly Burnham * William S. Peters, Sr.

November Feature Poets
Jocelyn Mosman * Jackie Allen * James Moore * Neville Hiatt

THE YEAR OF THE POET
December 2014

The Poetry Posse
Jamie Bond
Gail Weston Shazor
Albert 'Infinite' Carrasco
Siddartha Beth Pierce
Janet P. Caldwell
June 'Bugg' Barefield
Debbie M. Allen
Tony Henninger
DaVerbal Minddancer
Robert Gibbons
Neetu Wali
Shareef Abdur-Rasheed
Kimberly Burnham
William S. Peters, Sr.

Narcissus

December Feature Poets
Katherine Wyatt * Writtenkitten * Santo Molino * Justice ...ne

Now Available

www.innerchildpress.com/the-year-of-the-poet

187

The Year of the Poet II
May 2015

May's Featured Poets

Geri Algeri
Akin Mosi Chinmere
Anna Jakubcza

Emeralds

The Poetry Posse 2015

Jamie Bond * Gail Weston Shazor * Albert 'Infinite' Carrasco
Siddartha Beth Pierce * Janet P. Caldwell * Tony Henninger
Joe DaVerbal Minddancer * Neetu Wali * Shareef Abdur – Rasheed
Kimberly Burnham * Ann White * Keith Alan Hamilton
Katherine Wyatt * Fahredin Shehu * Hülya N. Yılmaz
Teresa E. Gallion * Jackie Allen * William S. Peters. Sr.

The Year of the Poet II
June 2015

June's Featured Poets

Aaahit Araonmyan * Yvette D. Murrell * Regina A. Walker

Pearl

The Poetry Posse 2015

Jamie Bond * Gail Weston Shazor * Albert 'Infinite' Carrasco
Siddartha Beth Pierce * Janet P. Caldwell * Tony Henninger
Joe DaVerbal Minddancer * Neetu Wali * Shareef Abdur – Rasheed
Kimberly Burnham * Ann White * Keith Alan Hamilton
Katherine Wyatt * Fahredin Shehu * Hülya N. Yılmaz
Teresa E. Gallion * Jackie Allen * William S. Peters. Sr.

The Year of the Poet II
July 2015

The Featured Poets for July 2015

Abhik Shome * Christina Neal * Robert Neal

Rubies

The Poetry Posse 2015

Jamie Bond * Gail Weston Shazor * Albert 'Infinite' Carrasco
Siddartha Beth Pierce * Janet P. Caldwell * Tony Henninger
Joe DaVerbal Minddancer * Neetu Wali * Shareef Abdur – Rasheed
Kimberly Burnham * Ann White * Keith Alan Hamilton
Katherine Wyatt * Fahredin Shehu * Hülya N. Yılmaz
Teresa E. Gallion * Jackie Allen * William S. Peters. Sr.

The Year of the Poet II
August 2015

Peridot

Featured Poets

Gayle Howell
Ann Chalasz
Christopher Schultz

The Poetry Posse 2015

Jamie Bond * Gail Weston Shazor * Albert 'Infinite' Carrasco
Siddartha Beth Pierce * Janet P. Caldwell * Tony Henninger
Joe DaVerbal Minddancer * Neetu Wali * Shareef Abdur – Rasheed
Kimberly Burnham * Ann White * Keith Alan Hamilton
Katherine Wyatt * Fahredin Shehu * Hülya N. Yılmaz
Teresa E. Gallion * Jackie Allen * William S. Peters. Sr.

Now Available

www.innerchildpress.com/the-year-of-the-poet

The Year of the Poet II
September 2015

Featured Poets
Alfreda Ghee | Lonneice Weeks Badley | Demetrios Trifiatis

Sapphires

The Poetry Posse 2015
Jamie Bond * Gail Weston Shazor * Albert 'Infinite' Carrasco
Siddartha Beth Pierce * Janet P. Caldwell * Tony Henninger
Joe DaVerbal Minddancer * Neetu Wali * Shareef Abdur – Rasheed
Kimberly Burnham * Ann White * Keith Alan Hamilton
Katherine Wyatt * Fahredin Shehu * Hülya N. Yılmaz
Teresa E. Gallion * Jackie Allen * William S. Peters, Sr.

The Year of the Poet II
October 2015

Featured Poets
Monte Smith * Laura J. Wolfe * William Washington

Opal

The Poetry Posse 2015
Jamie Bond * Gail Weston Shazor * Albert 'Infinite' Carrasco
Siddartha Beth Pierce * Janet P. Caldwell * Tony Henninger
Joe DaVerbal Minddancer * Neetu Wali * Shareef Abdur – Rasheed
Kimberly Burnham * Ann White * Keith Alan Hamilton
Katherine Wyatt * Fahredin Shehu * Hülya N. Yılmaz
Teresa E. Gallion * Jackie Allen * William S. Peters, Sr.

The Year of the Poet II
November 2015

Featured Poets
Alan W. Jankowski
Bismay Mohanty
James Mosse

Topaz

The Poetry Posse 2015
Jamie Bond * Gail Weston Shazor * Albert 'Infinite' Carrasco
Siddartha Beth Pierce * Janet P. Caldwell * Tony Henninger
Joe DaVerbal Minddancer * Neetu Wali * Shareef Abdur – Rasheed
Kimberly Burnham * Ann White * Keith Alan Hamilton
Katherine Wyatt * Fahredin Shehu * Hülya N. Yılmaz
Teresa E. Gallion * Jackie Allen * William S. Peters, Sr.

The Year of the Poet II
December 2015

Featured Poets
Kerione Bryan * Michelle Joan Barulich * Neville Hiatt

Turquoise

The Poetry Posse 2015
Jamie Bond * Gail Weston Shazor * Albert 'Infinite' Carrasco
Siddartha Beth Pierce * Janet P. Caldwell * Tony Henninger
Joe DaVerbal Minddancer * Neetu Wali * Shareef Abdur – Rasheed
Kimberly Burnham * Ann White * Keith Alan Hamilton
Katherine Wyatt * Fahredin Shehu * Hülya N. Yılmaz
Teresa E. Gallion * Jackie Allen * William S. Peters, Sr.

Now Available

www.innerchildpress.com/the-year-of-the-poet

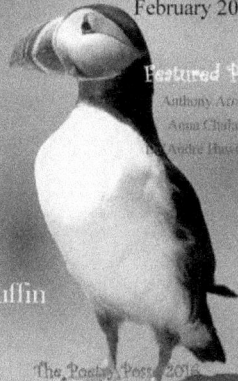

Now Available

www.innerchildpress.com/the-year-of-the-poet

The Year of the Poet
May 2016

Bob Strum
Barbara Allan
D.L. Davis

Oriole

The Year of the Poet III
June 2016

Featured Poets

Qibrije Demiri- Frangu
Naime Beqiraj
Faleeha Hassan
Bedri Zyberaj

Black Necked Stilt

The Poetry Posse 2016

Tram Fatima 'Ashi
Langley Shazor
Jody Doty
Emilia T. Davis

Indigo Bunting

The Poetry Posse 2016

The Year of the Poet III
August 2016

Featured Poets

Anita Dash
Irena Jovanovic
Malgorzata Gouluda

Painted Bunting

The Poetry Posse 2016

Now Available

www.innerchildpress.com/the-year-of-the-poet

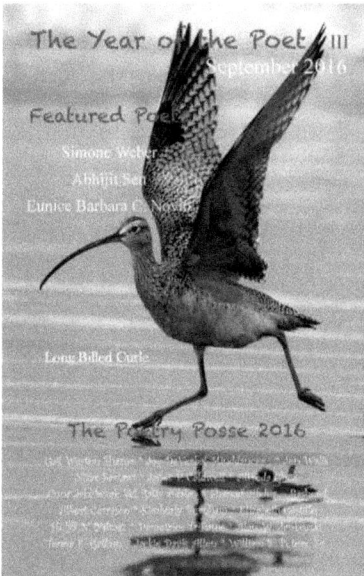

The Year of the Poet III
September 2016

Featured Poets

Simone Weber
Abhijit Sen
Eunice Barbara C. Novio

Long Billed Curle

The Poetry Posse 2016

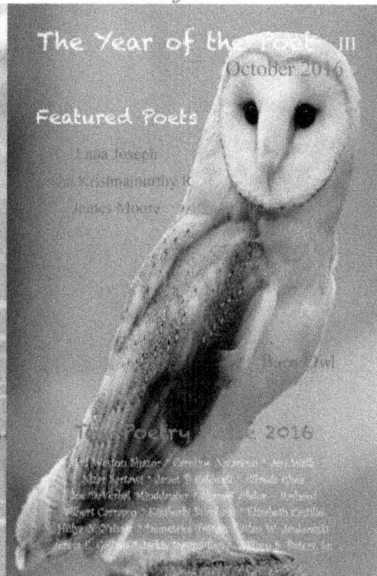

The Year of the Poet III
October 2016

Featured Poets

Lina Joseph
Krishnamurthy
James Moore

The Poetry Posse 2016

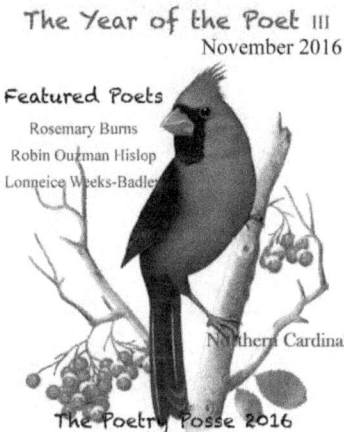

The Year of the Poet III
November 2016

Featured Poets

Rosemary Burns
Robin Ouzman Hislop
Lonneice Weeks-Badler

Northern Cardinal

The Poetry Posse 2016

Gail Weston Shazor * Caroline Nazareno * Jen Walls
Neetu Sarpaet * Janet P. Caldwell * Hülya Çhen
Joe DeVerial Middibraces * Shareef Abdur – Rasheed
Albert Carrasco * Kimberly Burnham * Elizabeth Castillo
Hülya N. Yılmaz * Demetrios Trifiath * Mjo W. Jankowski
Teresa E. Gallion * Jackie Davis Allen * William S. Peters, Sr.

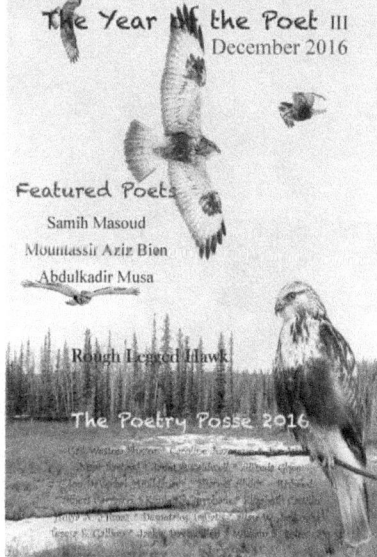

The Year of the Poet III
December 2016

Featured Poets

Samih Masoud
Mountassir Aziz Bion
Abdulkadir Musa

Rough Legged Hawk

The Poetry Posse 2016

Now Available

www.innerchildpress.com/the-year-of-the-poet

The Year of the Poet IV
January 2017

Featured Poets

Jen Winell
Natalie Shields
Irani Fatima Asad

Quaking Aspen

The Poetry Posse 2017

Gail Weston Shazor * Caroline Nazareno * Shinay Mohruti
Nizar Sartawi * Jhuse Jakubczak Val Betty Adelari * Jen Wells
Joe DeVerbal Minddancer * Shareef Abdur - Rasheed
Albert Carrasco * Kimberly Burnham * Elizabeth Castillo
Hülya N. Yılmaz * Teloeba Hanson * Alan W. Jankowski
Teresa E. Gallion * Jackie Davis Allen * William S. Peters, Sr.

The Year of the Poet IV
February 2017

Featured Poets

Lin Ross
Soukaina Fathi
Anwer Ghani

Witch Hazel

The Poetry Posse 2017

Gail Weston Shazor * Caroline Nazareno * Shinay Mohruti
Nizar Sartawi * Jhuse Jakubczak Val Betty Adelari * Jen Wells
Joe DeVerbal Minddancer * Shareef Abdur - Rasheed
Albert Carrasco * Kimberly Burnham * Elizabeth Castillo
Hülya N. Yılmaz * Teloeba Hanson * Alan W. Jankowski
Teresa E. Gallion * Jackie Davis Allen * William S. Peters, Sr.

The Year of the Poet IV
March 2017

Featured Poets

Tremell Stevens
Francisca Ricinski
Jamil Abu Shaih

The Eastern Redbud

The Poetry Posse 2017

Gail Weston Shazor * Caroline Nazareno * Shinay Mohruti
Teresa E. Gallion * Jhuse Jakubczak Val Betty Adelari
Joe DeVerbal Minddancer * Shareef Abdur - Rasheed
Albert Carrasco * Kimberly Burnham * Elizabeth Castillo
Hülya N. Yılmaz * Teloeba Hanson * Jackie Davis Allen
Jen Wells * Nizar Sartawi * * William S. Peters, Sr.

The Year of the Poet IV
April 2017

Featured Poets

Dr. Ruchida Barman
Neptune Barman
Masood Khalaf

The Blossoming Cherry

The Poetry Posse 2017

Gail Weston Shazor * Caroline Nazareno * Shinay Mohruti

Now Available

www.innerchildpress.com/the-year-of-the-poet

194

The Year of the Poet IV
May 2017

The Flowering Dogwood Tree

Featured Poets
Kallisa Powell
Alicja Maria Kuberska
Fethi Sassi

The Poetry Posse 2017

Gail Weston Shazor * Caroline Nazareno * Ranny Mohanty
Teresa E. Gallion * Jhuna Jakubczak Val Batty Ndabo
Joe DeVerhol Minddancer * Shareef Abdur – Rasheed
Albert Carrasco * Kimberly Burnham * Elizabeth Castillo
Hülya N Yılmaz * Felasche Hassan * Jackie Davis Allen
Jen Walls * Nizar Sartawi * * William S. Peters, Sr.

The Year of the Poet IV
June 2017

Featured Poets
Eliza Segiet
Tze-Min Tsai
Abdulla Issa

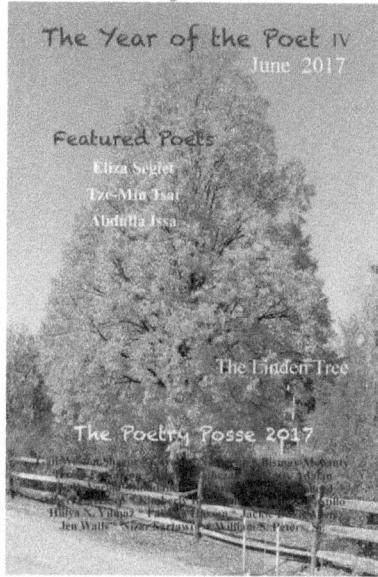

The Linden Tree

The Poetry Posse 2017

Ranny Mohanty
Val Batty Ndabo

Hülya N Yılmaz
Jen Walls * Nizar Sartawi * William S. Peters

The Year of the Poet IV
July 2017

Featured Poets
Anca Mihaela Bruma
Ibaa Ismail
Zvonko Taneski

The Oak Moon

The Poetry Posse 2017

The Year of the Poet IV
August 2017

Featured Poets
Jonathan Aquino
Kitty Hsu
Langley Shazor

The Hazelnut Tree

The Poetry Posse 2017

Gail Weston Shazor * Caroline Nazareno *
Teresa E. Gallion * Jhuna Jakubczak Val Batty Ndabo
Joe DeVerhol Minddancer * Shareef Abdur – Rasheed
Albert Carrasco * Kimberly Burnham * Elizabeth Castillo
Hülya N Yılmaz * Felasche Hassan * Jackie Davis Allen
Jen Walls * Nizar Sartawi * * William S. Peters, Sr.

Now Available

www.innerchildpress.com/the-year-of-the-poet

The Year of the Poet IV
September 2017

Featured Poets

Martina Reisz Newberry

Ameer Nassir

Christine Fulco Neal

Robert Neal

The Elm Tree

The Poetry Posse 2017

Gail Weston Shazor * Caroline Nazareno * Bismay Mohanty
Teresa E. Gallion * Anna Jakubczak Vel Ratty Adalan
Joe DaVerbal Minddancer * Shareef Abdur – Rasheed
Albert Carrasco * Kimberly Burnham * Elizabeth Castillo
Hülya N. Yılmaz * Faleeha Hassan * Jackie Davis Allen
Jen Walls * Nizar Sartawi * * William S. Peters, Sr.

The Year of the Poet IV
October 2017

Featured Poets

Ahmed Abu Saleem

Nedal Al-Qaeim

Sadeddin Shahin

The Black Walnut Tree

The Poetry Posse 2017

Gail Weston Shazor * Caroline Nazareno * Bismay Mohanty
Teresa E. Gallion * Anna Jakubczak Vel Ratty Adalan
Joe DaVerbal Minddancer * Shareef Abdur – Rasheed
Albert Carrasco * Kimberly Burnham * Elizabeth Castillo
Hülya N. Yılmaz * Faleeha Hassan * Jackie Davis Allen
Jen Walls * Nizar Sartawi * * William S. Peters, Sr.

The Year of the Poet IV
November 2017

Featured Poets

Kay Peters

Alfreda D. Ghee

Gabriella Garofalo

Rosemary Cappello

The Tree of Life

The Poetry Posse 2017

Gail Weston Shazor * Caroline Nazareno * Bismay Mohanty
Teresa E. Gallion * Anna Jakubczak Vel Ratty Adalan
Joe DaVerbal Minddancer * Shareef Abdur – Rasheed
Albert Carrasco * Kimberly Burnham * Elizabeth Castillo
Hülya N. Yılmaz * Faleeha Hassan * Jackie Davis Allen
Jen Walls * Nizar Sartawi * William S. Peters, Sr.

The Year of the Poet IV
December 2017

Featured Poets

Justice Clarke

Mariel M. Pabroa

Kiley Brown

The Fig Tree

The Poetry Posse 2017

Gail Weston Shazor * Caroline Nazareno * Bismay Mohanty
Teresa E. Gallion * Anna Jakubczak Vel Ratty Adalan
Joe DaVerbal Minddancer * Shareef Abdur – Rasheed
Albert Carrasco * Kimberly Burnham * Elizabeth Castillo
Hülya N. Yılmaz * Faleeha Hassan * Jackie Davis Allen
Jen Walls * Nizar Sartawi * William S. Peters, Sr.

Now Available

www.innerchildpress.com/the-year-of-the-poet

Now Available

www.innerchildpress.com/the-year-of-the-poet

The Year of the Poet V
May 2018

Featured Poets

Paddy Carisoan de Leeuch
Sylwia K. Malinowska
Landisz Abraats
Ofelia Pashin

The Sumerians

The Poetry Posse 2018

Gail Weston Shazor * Nizar Sartawi * Hülya N. Yilmaz
Jackie Davis Allen * Caroline 'Ceri' Nazareno
Alicja Maria Kuberska * Teresa E. Gallion
Kimberly Burnham * Shareef Abdur – Rasheed
Faleeha Hassan * Elizabeth Castillo * Swapna Behera
Tezmin Ition Tsai * William S. Peters, Sr.

The Year of the Poet V
June 2018

Featured Poets

Bilall Maliqi * Daim Miftari * Gojko Božović * Sofija Živković

The Paleo Indians

The Poetry Posse 2018

Gail Weston Shazor * Nizar Sartawi * Hülya N. Yilmaz
Jackie Davis Allen * Caroline 'Ceri' Nazareno
Alicja Maria Kuberska * Teresa E. Gallion
Kimberly Burnham * Shareef Abdur – Rasheed
Faleeha Hassan * Elizabeth Castillo * Swapna Behera
Tezmin Ition Tsai * William S. Peters, Sr.

The Year of the Poet V
July 2018

Featured Poets
Fabball Irengar-Paddy
Mohammad Iqbal Hariri
Eliza Segiet
Tom Higgins

Oceania

The Poetry Posse 2018

Gail Weston Shazor * Nizar Sartawi * Hülya N. Yilmaz
Jackie Davis Allen * Caroline 'Ceri' Nazareno
Alicja Maria Kuberska * Teresa E. Gallion
Kimberly Burnham * Shareef Abdur – Rasheed
Faleeha Hassan * Elizabeth Castillo * Swapna Behera
Tezmin Ition Tsai * William S. Peters, Sr.

The Year of the Poet V
August 2018

Featured Poets
Hussein Habasch * Mircea Dan Duta * Naida Mujkić * Swagni Das

The Lapita

The Poetry Posse 2018

Gail Weston Shazor * Nizar Sartawi * Hülya N. Yilmaz
Jackie Davis Allen * Caroline 'Ceri' Nazareno
Alicja Maria Kuberska * Teresa E. Gallion
Kimberly Burnham * Shareef Abdur – Rasheed
Ashok K. Bhargava* Elizabeth Castillo * Swapna Behaera
Tezmin Ition Tsai * William S. Peters, Sr.

Now Available

www.innerchildpress.com/the-year-of-the-poet

The Year of the Poet V

September 2018

The Aztecs & Incas

Featured Poets

Kolade Olanrewaju Freedom
Eliza Segiet
Moshiej Hussain Abdul Ghani
Lily Swarn

The Poetry Posse 2018

Gail Weston Shazor * Nizar Sartawi * Hülya N. Yılmaz
Jackie Davis Allen * Caroline 'Ceri' Nazareno
Alicja Maria Kuberska * Teresa E. Gallion
Kimberly Burnham * Shareef Abdur – Rasheed
Ashok K. Bhargava * Elizabeth Castillo * Swapna Behera
Tezmin Ition Tsai * William S. Peters, Sr.

The Year of the Poet V

October 2018

Featured Poets

Alicia Minjarez * Lonneice Weeks-Badley
Lopamudra Mishra * Abdelwahed Souayah

The Poetry Posse 2018

Gail Weston Shazor * Nizar Sartawi * Hülya N. Yılmaz
Jackie Davis Allen * Caroline 'Ceri' Nazareno
Alicja Maria Kuberska * Teresa E. Gallion
Kimberly Burnham * Shareef Abdur – Rasheed
Ashok K. Bhargava * Elizabeth Castillo * Swapna Behera
Tezmin Ition Tsai * William S. Peters, Sr.

The Year of the Poet V

November 2018

Featured Poets

Michelle Joan Barulich * Monsif Beroual
Krystyna Konecka * Nassira Nezzar

The Poetry Posse 2018

Gail Weston Shazor * Nizar Sartawi * Hülya N. Yılmaz
Jackie Davis Allen * Caroline 'Ceri' Nazareno
Alicja Maria Kuberska * Teresa E. Gallion
Kimberly Burnham * Shareef Abdur – Rasheed
Ashok K. Bhargava * Elizabeth Castillo * Swapna Behera
Tezmin Ition Tsai * William S. Peters, Sr.

The Year of the Poet V

December 2018

Featured Poets

Rose Terranova Cirigliano
Joanna Kalinowska
Sokolović Emin
Dr. T. Ashok Chakravarthy

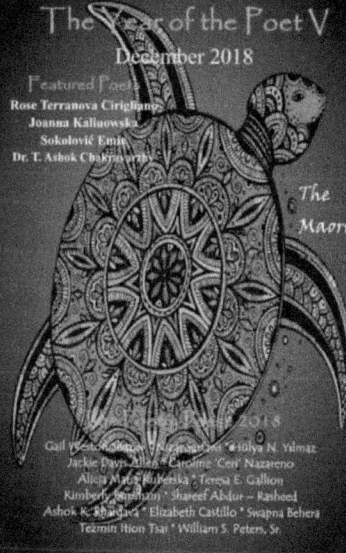

The Poetry Posse 2018

Gail Weston Shazor * Nizar Sartawi * Hülya N. Yılmaz
Jackie Davis Allen * Caroline 'Ceri' Nazareno
Alicja Maria Kuberska * Teresa E. Gallion
Kimberly Burnham * Shareef Abdur – Rasheed
Ashok K. Bhargava * Elizabeth Castillo * Swapna Behera
Tezmin Ition Tsai * William S. Peters, Sr.

Now Available

www.innerchildpress.com/the-year-of-the-poet

Inner Child Press Anthologies

The Year of the Poet VI
January 2019

Indigenous North Americans

Featured Poets

Houda Elfchtali
Anthony Briscoe
Iram Fatima 'Ashi'
Dr. K. K. Mathew

Dream Catcher

The Poetry Posse 2019

Gail Weston Shazor * Joe Paire * Hülya N. Yılmaz
Jackie Davis Allen * Caroline Ceın Nazareno
Alicja Maria Kubenska * Teresa E. Gallion
Kimberly Burnham * Shareef Abdur – Rasheed
Ashok K. Bhargava * Elizabeth Castillo * Swapna Behera
Tezmin Ition Tsai * William S. Peters, Sr

The Year of the Poet VI
February 2019

Featured Poets

Marek Lukaszewicz * Bharati Nayak
Aida G. Roque * Jean-Jacques Fournier

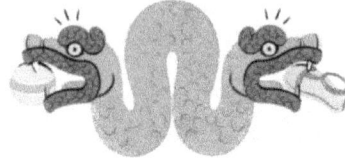

Meso-America

The Poetry Posse 2019

Gail Weston Shazor * Albert Carrasco * Hülya N. Yılmaz
Jackie Davis Allen * Caroline Nazareno * Eliza Segiet
Alicja Maria Kubenska * Teresa E. Gallion * Joe Paire
Kimberly Burnham * Shareef Abdur – Rasheed
Ashok K. Bhargava * Elizabeth Castillo * Swapna Behera
Tezmin Ition Tsai * William S. Peters, Sr.

The Year of the Poet VI
March 2019

Featured Poets

Enesa Mahmić * Sylwia K. Malinowska
Sharook Hammoud * Anwer Ghani

The Caribbean

The Poetry Posse 2019

Gail Weston Shazor * Albert Carrasco * Hülya N. Yılmaz
Jackie Davis Allen * Caroline Nazareno * Eliza Segiet
Alicja Maria Kubenska * Teresa E. Gallion * Joe Paire
Kimberly Burnham * Shareef Abdur – Rasheed
Ashok K. Bhargava * Elizabeth Castillo * Swapna Behera
Tezmin Ition Tsai * William S. Peters, Sr.

The Year of the Poet VI
April 2019

Featured Poets

DL Davis * Michelle Joan Barulich
Lulëzim Haziri * Faleeha Hassan

Central & West Africa

The Poetry Posse 2019

Gail Weston Shazor * Albert Carrasco * Hülya N. Yılmaz
Jackie Davis Allen * Caroline Nazareno * Eliza Segiet
Alicja Maria Kubenska * Teresa E. Gallion * Joe Paire
Kimberly Burnham * Shareef Abdur – Rasheed
Ashok K. Bhargava * Elizabeth Castillo * Swapna Behera
Tezmin Ition Tsai * William S. Peters, Sr.

Now Available

www.innerchildpress.com/the-year-of-the-poet

The Year of the Poet VI
May 2019

Featured Poets

Emad Al-Haydary * Hussein Nasser Jabr
Wahab Sheriff * Abdul Razzaq Al Ameeri

Asia Southeast Asia and Maritime Asia

The Poetry Posse 2019

Gail Weston Shazor * Albert Carrasco * Hülya N. Yılmaz
Jackie Davis Allen * Caroline Nazareno * Eliza Segiet
Alicja Maria Kubolska * Teresa E. Gallion * Joe Paire
Kimberly Burnham * Shareef Abdur – Rasheed
Ashok K. Bhargava * Elizabeth Castillo * Swapna Behera
Tezmin Ition Tsai * William S. Peters, Sr.

The Year of the Poet VI
June 2019

Featured Poets

Kate Gaudi Powiekszone * Sahaj Sabharwal
Iwu Jeff * Mohamed Abdel Aziz Shmeis

Arctic
Circumpolar

The Poetry Posse 2019

Gail Weston Shazor * Albert Carrasco * Hülya N. Yılmaz
Jackie Davis Allen * Caroline Nazareno * Eliza Segiet
Alicja Maria Kubolska * Teresa E. Gallion * Joe Paire
Kimberly Burnham * Shareef Abdur – Rasheed
Ashok K. Bhargava * Elizabeth Castillo * Swapna Behera
Tezmin Ition Tsai * William S. Peters, Sr.

The Year of the Poet VI

Featured Poets

Shahieddin Shahin * Andy Scott
Fehryein Sushu * Alok Kumar Ray

The Horn of Africa

Ethiopia   Djibouti

Somalia   Eritrea

The Poetry Posse 2019

Gail Weston Shazor * Albert Carrasco * Hülya N. Yılmaz
Jackie Davis Allen * Caroline Nazareno * Eliza Segiet
Alicja Maria Kubolska * Teresa E. Gallion * Joe Paire
Kimberly Burnham * Shareef Abdur – Rasheed
Ashok K. Bhargava * Elizabeth Castillo * Swapna Behera
Tezmin Ition Tsai * William S. Peters, Sr.

The Year of the Poet VI
August 2019

Featured Poets

Shola Balogun * Bharati Nayak
Monalisa Dash Dwibedy * Mbizo Chirasha

Coexist

Southwest Asia

The Poetry Posse 2019

Gail Weston Shazor * Albert Carrasco * Hülya N. Yılmaz
Jackie Davis Allen * Caroline Nazareno * Eliza Segiet
Alicja Maria Kubolska * Teresa E. Gallion * Joe Paire
Kimberly Burnham * Shareef Abdur – Rasheed
Ashok K. Bhargava * Elizabeth Castillo * Swapna Behera
Tezmin Ition Tsai * William S. Peters, Sr.

Now Available

www.innerchildpress.com/the-year-of-the-poet

The Year of the Poet VI

September 2019

Featured Poets
Elena Liliana Popescu * Gobinda Biswas
Irom Fatima 'Ashi' * Joseph S. Spence, Sr

The Caucasus
The Poetry Posse 2019

Gail Weston Shazor * Albert Carrasco * Hülya N. Yılmaz
Jackie Davis Allen * Caroline Nazareno * Eliza Segiet
Alicja Maria Kuberska * Teresa E. Gallion * Joe Paire
Kimberly Burnham * shareef Abdur – Rasheed
Ashok K. Bhargava * Elizabeth Castillo * Swapna Behera
Tezmin Ition Tsai * William S. Peters, Sr.

The Year of the Poet VI

October 2019

Featured Poets
Ngozi Olivia Osuoha * Denisa Kondić
Pankhuri Sinha * Christena AV Williams

The Nile Valley
The Poetry Posse 2019

Gail Weston Shazor * Albert Carrasco * Hülya N. Yılmaz
Jackie Davis Allen * Caroline Nazareno * Eliza Segiet
Alicja Maria Kuberska * Teresa E. Gallion * Joe Paire
Kimberly Burnham * shareef Abdur – Rasheed
Ashok K. Bhargava * Elizabeth Castillo * Swapna Behera
Tezmin Ition Tsai * William S. Peters, Sr.

The Year of the Poet VI

November 2019

Featured Poets
Rozalie Aleksandrova * Orbindu Ganga
Smruti Ranjan Mohanty * Sofia Skleida

Northern Asia
The Poetry Posse 2019

Gail Weston Shazor * Albert Carrasco * Hülya N. Yılmaz
Jackie Davis Allen * Caroline Nazareno * Eliza Segiet
Alicja Maria Kuberska * Teresa E. Gallion * Joe Paire
Kimberly Burnham * shareef Abdur – Rasheed
Ashok K. Bhargava * Elizabeth Castillo * Swapna Behera
Tezmin Ition Tsai * William S. Peters, Sr.

The Year of the Poet VI

December 2019

Featured Poets
Kalura Kanon Chorneanu * Sujata Paul
Bhaswati Nayak * Kapardeli Eftichia

Oceania
The Poetry Posse 2019

Gail Weston Shazor * Albert Carrasco * Hülya N. Yılmaz
Jackie Davis Allen * Caroline Nazareno * Eliza Segiet
Alicja Maria Kuberska * Teresa E. Gallion * Joe Paire
Kimberly Burnham * shareef Abdur – Rasheed
Ashok K. Bhargava * Elizabeth Castillo * Swapna Behera
Tezmin Ition Tsai * William S. Peters, Sr.

Now Available

www.innerchildpress.com/the-year-of-the-poet

The Year of the Poet VII
January 2020
Featured Poets
B S Tyagi * Ashok Chakravarthy Tholana
Andy Scott * Anwer Ghani

1901 Jean Henry Dunant and Frédéric Passy

The Year of Peace
Celebrating past Nobel Peace Prize Recipients

The Poetry Posse 2020
Gail Weston Shazor * Albert Carasco * Hülya N. Yılmaz
Jackie Davis Allen * Caroline Nazareno * Eliza Segiet
Alicja Maria Kuberska * Teresa E. Gallion * Joe Paire
Kimberly Burnham * Shareef Abdur – Rasheed
Ashok K. Bhargava * Elizabeth Castillo * Swapna Behera
Tezmin Ition Tsai * William S. Peters, Sr.

The Year of the Poet VII
February 2020
Featured Poets
Jennifer Ades * Martina Reisz Newberry
Ibrahim Honjo * Claudia Piccinno

Henri La Fontaine ~ 1913

The Year of Peace
Celebrating past Nobel Peace Prize Recipients

The Poetry Posse 2020
Gail Weston Shazor * Albert Carasco * Hülya N. Yılmaz
Jackie Davis Allen * Caroline Nazareno * Eliza Segiet
Alicja Maria Kuberska * Teresa E. Gallion * Joe Paire
Kimberly Burnham * Shareef Abdur – Rasheed
Ashok K. Bhargava * Elizabeth Castillo * Swapna Behera
Tezmin Ition Tsai * William S. Peters, Sr.

The Year of the Poet VII
March 2020
Featured Poets
Aziz Mountassir * Krishna Paraisa
Hannie Rouweler * Rozalia Aleksandrova

Aristide Briand ~ 1926 ~ Gustav Stresemann

The Year of Peace
Celebrating past Nobel Peace Prize Recipients

The Poetry Posse 2020
Gail Weston Shazor * Albert Carasco * Hülya N. Yılmaz
Jackie Davis Allen * Caroline Nazareno * Eliza Segiet
Alicja Maria Kuberska * Teresa E. Gallion * Joe Paire
Kimberly Burnham * Shareef Abdur – Rasheed
Ashok K. Bhargava * Elizabeth Castillo * Swapna Behera
Tezmin Ition Tsai * William S. Peters, Sr.

The Year of the Poet VII
April 2020
Featured Poets
Rohini Behera * Mircea Dan Duta
Monalisa Dash Dwibedy * NilavroNill Shoovro

Carlos Saavedra Lamas ~ 1936

The Year of Peace
Celebrating past Nobel Peace Prize Recipients

The Poetry Posse 2020
Gail Weston Shazor * Albert Carasco * Hülya N. Yılmaz
Jackie Davis Allen * Caroline Nazareno * Eliza Segiet
Alicja Maria Kuberska * Teresa E. Gallion * Joe Paire
Kimberly Burnham * Shareef Abdur – Rasheed
Ashok K. Bhargava * Elizabeth Castillo * Swapna Behera
Tezmin Ition Tsai * William S. Peters, Sr.

Now Available

www.innerchildpress.com/the-year-of-the-poet

The Year of the Poet VII
May 2020

Featured Poets
Alok Kumar Ray * Eden S. Trinidad
Franco Barbato * Izabela Zubko

Ralph Bunche ~ 1950

The Year of Peace
Celebrating past Nobel Peace Prize Recipients

The Poetry Posse 2020
Gail Weston Shazor * Albert Carasco * Hülya N. Yılmaz
Jackie Davis Allen * Caroline Nazareno * Eliza Segiet
Alicja Maria Kuberska * Teresa E. Gallion * Joe Paire
Kimberly Burnham * Shareef Abdur – Rasheed
Ashok K. Bhargava * Elizabeth Castillo * Swapna Behera
Tezmin Ition Tsai * William S. Peters, Sr.

The Year of the Poet VII
June 2020

Featured Poets
Eftichia Kapardeli * Metin Cengiz
Hussein Habasch * Kosh K Mathew

Albert John Lutuli ~ 1960

The Year of Peace
Celebrating past Nobel Peace Prize Recipients

The Poetry Posse 2020
Gail Weston Shazor * Albert Carasco * Hülya N. Yılmaz
Jackie Davis Allen * Caroline Nazareno * Eliza Segiet
Alicja Maria Kuberska * Teresa E. Gallion * Joe Paire
Kimberly Burnham * Shareef Abdur – Rasheed
Ashok K. Bhargava * Elizabeth Castillo * Swapna Behera
Tezmin Ition Tsai * William S. Peters, Sr

The Year of the Poet VII
July 2020

Featured Poets
Mykola Martyniuk * Orbindu Ganga
Roula Pollard * Kam Praktisha

Norman Ernest Borlaug ~ 1970

The Year of Peace
Celebrating past Nobel Peace Prize Recipients

The Poetry Posse 2020
Gail Weston Shazor * Albert Carasco * Hülya N. Yılmaz
Jackie Davis Allen * Caroline Nazareno * Eliza Segiet
Alicja Maria Kuberska * Teresa E. Gallion * Joe Paire
Kimberly Burnham * Shareef Abdur – Rasheed
Ashok K. Bhargava * Elizabeth Castillo * Swapna Behera
Tezmin Ition Tsai * William S. Peters, Sr

The Year of the Poet VII
August 2020

Featured Poets
Dr Pragya Suman * Chinh Nguyen
Srinivas Vasudev * Ugwu Leonard Ifeanyi, Jr.

Adolfo Pérez Esquivel ~ 1980

The Year of Peace
Celebrating past Nobel Peace Prize Recipients

The Poetry Posse 2020
Gail Weston Shazor * Albert Carasco * Hülya N. Yılmaz
Jackie Davis Allen * Caroline Nazareno * Eliza Segiet
Alicja Maria Kuberska * Teresa E. Gallion * Joe Paire
Kimberly Burnham * Shareef Abdur – Rasheed
Ashok K. Bhargava * Elizabeth Castillo * Swapna Behera
Tezmin Ition Tsai * William S. Peters, Sr

Now Available

www.innerchildpress.com/the-year-of-the-poet

The Year of the Poet VII
September 2020
Featured Poets
Raed Anis Al-Jishi • Isolazione Slovenia
Dr. Haqesh Kumar Gupta • Umid Najjari
Mikhail Sergeyevich Gorbachev ~ 1990

The Year of Peace
Celebrating past Nobel Peace Prize Recipients
The Poetry Posse 2020

The Year of the Poet VII
October 2020
Featured Poets
Mutawaf A. Shaheed • Galina Italvanskaya
Nadeem Fraz • Avril Tanya Meallem
Kim Dae-jung ~ 2000

The Year of Peace
Celebrating past Nobel Peace Prize Recipients
The Poetry Posse 2020

The Year of the Poet VII
November 2020
Featured Poets
Elisa Mascia • Sue Lindenberg McClelland
Hanif Jacobs • Ivan Gacina
Liu Xiaobo ~ 2010

The Year of Peace
Celebrating past Nobel Peace Prize Recipients
The Poetry Posse 2020

The Year of the Poet VII
December 2020
Featured Poets
Ratan Ghosh • Ibtisam Ibrahim Al-Asady
Brindha Vinodh • Selma Kopic
Abiy Ahmed Ali ~ 2019

The Year of Peace
Celebrating past Nobel Peace Prize Recipients
The Poetry Posse 2020
Gail Weston Shazor • Albert Carrasco • Hülya N. Yılmaz
Jackie Davis Allen • Caroline Nazareno • Eliza Segiet
Alicja Maria Kuberska • Teresa E. Gallion • Joe Paire
Kimberly Burnham • Shareef Abdur - Rasheed
Ashok K. Bhargava • Elizabeth Castillo • Swapna Behera
Tezmin Htion Tsai • William S. Peters, Sr.

Now Available

www.innerchildpress.com/the-year-of-the-poet

and there is much, much more !

visit . . .

www.innerchildpress.com/antho
logies-sales-special.php

Also check out our Authors and
all the wonderful Books
Available at :

www.innerchildpress.com/autho
rs-pages

World Healing World Peace
2020

Poets for Humanity

Now Available

www.worldhealingworldpeacepoetry.com

INNER CHILD PRESS

WORLD HEALING WORLD PEACE
2018

A Poetry Anthology for Humanity

Now Available

www.worldhealingworldpeacepoetry.com

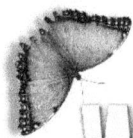

World Healing World Peace

support

www.worldhealingworldpeacepoetry.com

209

World Healing World Peace

2012, 2014, 2016, 2018, 2020

Now Available

www.worldhealingworldpeacepoetry.com

Inner Child Press International

'building bridges of cultural understanding'

Meet our Cultural Ambassadors

Fahredin Shehu
Director of Cultural

Faleha Hassan
Iraq – USA

Elizabeth E. Castillo
Philippines

Antoinette Coleman
Chicago
Midwest USA

Ananda Nepali
Nepal – Tibet
Northern India

Kimberly Burnham
Pacific Northwest
USA

Alicja Kuberska
Poland
Eastern Europe

Swapna Behera
India
Southeast Asia

Kolade O. Freedom
Nigeria
West Africa

Monsif Beroual
Morocco
Nothern Africa

Ashok K. Bhargava
Canada

Tzemin Ition Tsai
Republic of China
Greater China

Alicia M. Ramírez
Mexico
Central America

Christena AV Williams
Jamaica
Caribbean

Louise Hudon
Eastern Canada

Aziz Mountassir
Morocco
Northern Africa

Shareef Abdur-Rasheed
Southeastern USA

Laure Charazac
France
Western Europe

Mohammad Ikbal Harb
Lebanon
Middle East

**Mohamed Abdel
Aziz Shmeis**
Egypt
Middle East

Hilary Mainga
Kenya
Eastern Africa

Josephus R. Johnson
Liberia

www.innerchildpress.com

This Anthological Publication
is underwritten solely by

Inner Child Press International

Inner Child Press is a Publishing Company
Founded and Operated by Writers. Our
personal publishing experiences provides
us an intimate understanding of the
sometimes daunting challenges Writers,
New and Seasoned may face in the
Business of Publishing and Marketing
their Creative "Written Work".

For more Information

Inner Child Press International

www.innerchildpress.com

'building bridges of cultural understanding'

202 Wiltree Court, State College, Pennsylvania 16801

www.innerchildpress.com

~ fini ~

www.ingramcontent.com/pod-product-compliance
Lightning Source LLC
LaVergne TN
LVHW051046080426
835508LV00019B/1730